Discover powerful and positive methods
for getting everything you ever wanted

When Adrian Calabrese's faithful car bit the dust, she was broke and had already maxed out seven credit cards. She went looking for her dream car anyway, and by the end of the day she was the proud owner of a shiny new Jeep Cherokee.

It was all because she had found the secret formula for getting what she wanted. Not long after that, money began flowing in her direction, and she paid off all her debts and her life turned around.

Now Adrian Calabrese shares her powerful method of applying ancient concepts of inner wisdom to everyday life. *How to Get Everything You Ever Wanted* will show you how you can begin immediately to get everything out of life that you have ever desired.

About the Author

Adrian Calabrese, Ph.D., Msc.D., C.H., holds a doctorate in Psychical Research, another in Metaphysics, and is a Certified Clinical Hypnotherapist. A psychic, channel, medium, psychic artist, holistic practitioner, inspirational speaker, and minister, she has worked extensively with intuitive and pastoral counseling, past life regression, and spiritual energy healing, and is the founder and director of the Metaphysical Center for Arts & Sciences and pastor of the Metaphysical Church of the Spirit. Her other talents include backgrounds in performance, art, and broadcasting.

To Write to the Author

If you wish to contact the author or would like more information about this book, please write to the author in care of Llewellyn Worldwide and we will forward your request. Both the author and publisher appreciate hearing from you and learning of your enjoyment of this book and how it has helped you. Llewellyn Worldwide cannot guarantee that every letter written to the author can be answered, but all will be forwarded. Please write to:

Adrian Calabrese, Ph.D.

℅ Llewellyn Worldwide

2143 Wooddale Drive, Dept. 1-56718-119-8

Woodbury, MN 55125-2989, U.S.A.

Please enclose a self-addressed stamped envelope for reply,
or $1.00 to cover costs. If outside U.S.A., enclose
international postal reply coupon.

Many of Llewellyn's authors have websites with additional information and resources. For more information, please visit our website at
http://www.llewellyn.com

Adrian Calabrese, Ph.D.

How to Get Everything You Ever Wanted

Complete Guide to Using Your Psychic Common Sense

Llewellyn Publications
Woodbury, Minnesota

First Edition
Seventh Printing, 2006

Book design and editing by Rebecca Zins
Cover design by William Merlin Cannon

Library of Congress Cataloging-in-Publication Data
Calabrese, Adrian.
    How to get everything you ever wanted: complete guide to using your psychic common sense / Adrian Calabrese.—1st ed.
        p.   cm.
    Includes bibliographical references and index.
    ISBN 13: 978-1-56718-119-7
    ISBN 10: 1-56718-119-8
    1. Self-realization—Psychic aspects.   2. Success—Psychic aspects.   3. New Thought—Psychic aspects.   I. Title.

BF1045.S44 C35 2000
131—dc21
                                                                                    00-030934

Llewellyn Worldwide does not participate in, endorse, or have any authority or responsibility concerning private business transactions between our authors and the public.
    All mail addressed to the author is forwarded but the publisher cannot, unless specifically instructed by the author, give out an address or phone number.

Llewellyn Publications
A Division of Llewellyn Worldwide, Ltd.
2143 Wooddale Drive, Dept. 1-56718-119-8
Woodbury, MN 55125-2989, U.S.A.
www.llewellyn.com
Llewellyn is a registered trademark of Llewellyn Worldwide, Ltd.

Printed in the United States of America on recycled paper

Dedicated to my parents,
Ann and Rudy Calabrese,
with love.

Contents

Contents

Acknowledgments

Where to begin? Why not at the top? I thank You, God, for guiding my soul to this moment and this task, and for the privilege of serving You and all You have created. And so it is!

Second only to Spirit, I thank the two most loved and cherished souls in my life, who have made my journey on Earth possible: my mom and dad, Ann and Rudy Calabrese. Through their deep love, I learned to believe in myself, and that I could be, do, and have all that my heart desired. I picked the best the Universe had to offer, and I am so very grateful that they picked me.

Of course, I would be remiss if I did not thank my unseen helpers in Spirit who have guided and nurtured me throughout the writing of this book, particularly my spirit guide, Roger Smythe, my teacher and friend, whose initial presence shocked the heck out of me and changed my life forever. To my angel, Gabriel, I offer my loving thanks, and I will continue, with your help, to "trumpet the word"! To those I love who have made the transition to Spirit—Marge Goering, whose loving friendship I will always treasure, who encouraged the best in me and made me feel smart, talented and capable, when I couldn't see anything worthwhile in myself, to Nani and the little child-soul, Gabriel, who together watched over this book from its spiritual inception, and who continue to guide all my writing efforts.

Here on the Earth plane there are so many to thank that I could write another book of nothing but thank-you's and call it "My Gratitude Journal," but here goes . . .

My heartfelt thanks to all those at Llewellyn who read my book and decided it was worth printing, and to all those who made it happen. I thank Barbara Wright and Nancy Mostad for guiding me through the first-time author process, and Bill Cannon and his team for the beautiful cover. My blessings and thanks, especially, to Becky Zins, my very insightful and uplifting editor.

This book would not have been written if were not for some very special people that God put in my path to show me the way. My loving thanks goes to Jeff Burnett and Loriann Ercan, my dearest friends, who have embraced and loved me through thick and thin, book and all. I love you guys, now and always. I thank my friend Steven Dolan, who made me promise him I would write a book, and here it is. My thanks to Becky Flora, "the instrument," who introduced me to a life of wonder and Spirit. Thanks to Holly Thomas for her input in the early writing phases, and Doris Foster, who typed, sweated, and prayed with me while we waited for the "right and perfect publisher," and to Lisa Mainetti Kane, who guided this book, and its author, gently and generously through its conceptual and formative stages.

My love and thanks go to my dear family and friends, especially Lynn Heuermann, who cheered me on from the very start and who stands behind me even when I'm a pain in the neck. Get ready to "go on the road," Lynn! To the members of the Metaphysical Church of the Spirit and Metaphysical Center for Arts & Sciences, my eternal thanks to all of you for your loyalty, inspiration, and devotion.

Finally, my gratitude goes to those whose stories are mentioned in this book, and to all of you, the readers, may you always get everything you ever wanted. Blessings to you.

Go in light, love, and peace. And so it is!

Introduction

About four years ago my trusty Chevy Celebrity bit the dust. I loved her. I even gave her a nickname, Silver Streak. She was my pal, getting me everywhere I needed to go in record time. But when she coughed up her last transmission, I knew it was time to say goodbye—only I had some major problems. First, I was teaching at five—count 'em, five—colleges and had to go from one to the other every day, five days a week. The second problem was money. I was broke. Third, I had no credit because I had maxed out about seven credit cards to their excruciating limits by charging my apartment rent on them. To make matters worse, the income from all my teaching jobs was less than half my total monthly debt. I didn't think any self-respecting car dealer would lend me a penny. Still, I had always dreamed of a shiny, black Jeep Cherokee. Undaunted by poverty, I decided to manifest a new car.

Now I had learned and read about this manifesting stuff. My metaphysical and psychic studies had covered this topic, but I didn't have any experience with it myself. I thought it looked doable on paper but not in real life. All of the books on the subject seemed vague and mysterious and I felt there had to be an easier way. So with my back against the proverbial wall, I was determined to give manifesting a try—my way.

Devising my own method, I found a logical and simple route to my goal. As part of my mental preparation, I saw myself driving that Jeep with a big smile on my face and money in my pocket. I found that changing my thoughts, feelings, and attitudes toward getting what I wanted made me feel powerful. Thinking that a physical, tangible source would help me focus my thoughts, I even put a picture of my dream car, cut from a magazine, in front of me while I meditated on it by candlelight. I took a series of positive steps, such as writing down my request, to reinforce my intention. I just downright decided that

I was going to get that car and I did everything I could—physically, psychically, and spiritually—to make it happen.

The next day, I visited my folks in upstate New York and we decided to go car "looking" on a whim. Not shopping, but looking, because we all knew the odds were stacked against me. Bravely I held true to my heart and by the end of that day, to my pleasant surprise, I was the proud owner of a brand new, shiny, black Jeep Cherokee.

Amazingly, knowing that I had no money, no credit, and no immediate potential for money, the car dealer gave me a loan with low monthly installments I could handle. My parents surprised me by helping with the down payment and presto—I had my dream car. All of the necessary elements just fell into place because I found the secret formula to getting what I wanted, and the time was right. Not bad for two days' work. How did I do it? I just had to do my part of the mind-body work and the Universe took care of the details.

It didn't stop there. I was on a roll. In no time I put my theory and practice into action and began to receive everything I wanted. Money started to flow in my direction. I was able to pay off all my debts, $30,000 worth, and my life turned around. I found that when I applied my method, it always worked. From parking spaces to apartments and money to men, everything started coming to me.

Far be it from me to hoard this secret. A year later, when I set up my metaphysical holistic practice, I began teaching others to do the same. Case after case was remarkable. My students were manifesting mates, money, cars, homes, and even good health. This thing was bigger than all of us! That's when I decided to take pen to paper.

You are reading the result. This book can help you to get all the things your heart desires. It's the old "If I can do it, you can do it" theory, and it is true. The method I have devised and recorded here will work for you. All you need is a little dedication and a lot of faith.

If you follow the steps in this book, there is no way you will *not* succeed. I have outlined the basics of attracting and drawing what you want into your life in a simple and clear form. If you follow these steps diligently, in no time you will be reaping the rewards of your efforts.

I have organized the book into three sections. Part I, What It's All About, explains the concept of manifesting. It will tell you why we humans make the choices we do, and how to make the best ones for yourself. In this section, you will learn how to find out what you *really* want. You will also understand the spiritual and practical history and background of manifesting.

Part II, How You Do It, is the real meat of this book. This section tells you how to begin your manifesting work by understanding your own psychic abilities, or what I call your psychic common sense. This part covers the basic elements of manifesting, and focuses on teaching you how to send your desired messages out into the Universe and program them for success. This part ends with the six-step easy method of manifesting, which is usable for a lifetime. The six-step method is included on the removable bookmark, which can be easily cut from the back cover of this book. Very handy! You can begin to get everything you want the moment you finish this section—but please, read the rest of the book! There's lots more to know.

Finally, Part III, Pulling Out All The Stops, will help you discover your hidden talents, creativity, and artistic ability, and how to use them to enhance your manifesting work for a final blast of energy. The book ends with a chapter chock full of great, practical affirmations that really, really work!

You and I are on a spiritual journey, as well as a physical one. Our lives were not meant to be difficult or painful. This Universe of ours has given us the innate, unseen power to change our lives for the better and achieve what we truly deserve: constant happiness. The first step toward getting to your joy involves your commitment to yourself, your soul, to gratefully receive all the gifts of a loving Spirit. Take that step—because you *can* have it all. You were meant to.

PART ONE

What It's All About

CHAPTER 1

Making It Happen

I'm about to ask you to do something you might not want to do. Muster all the faith you can, and give it a try. I'm asking you to believe in magic. Yes, magic. Not the hocus-pocus kind, but the kind of magic that is locked inside the hearts and minds of us all—that hidden inner power we all possess that can help us to make the most of our lives and get everything we ever wanted.

At this point, you're probably thinking, "This woman is crazy. Doesn't she realize that some of us just can't ever get what we want? It's just not possible for all of us to have everything." Well, I'm challenging you to let go of that negative thinking, and start to believe that all things are possible.

It is true that we don't always know what we want, and that's the reason why we don't get it. You've got to be sure what your heart's desires are so that you can make them happen in your life. Start to believe that you can have what you want and that you have the power right there within you to do it.

Within you lies the secret of your dreams, the hidden strength to perform miracles. We all have this gift from birth; the trouble is, most of us don't know about it, and the rest of us are afraid of it. We have powerful spiritual and intuitive reserves that, when recognized, understood, and utilized to their greatest capacity, can dispel our fears and help us get the things we want out of life. But our fears may be strong enough to stop us. We're afraid that if we get what we ask for we won't be able to handle it emotionally, or worse, we won't be able to keep it.

For instance, you may ask for and manifest romantic love and marriage. Years or maybe even months down the road it gets rocky and the solidity of the relationship becomes shaky. The two of you are fighting or growing apart and eventually your marriage ends in divorce. You obviously got what you wanted but were unable to keep it and you now suffer the emotional pain of it all. *What you might not realize is that your happiness and success depend upon knowing what you truly want and how to ask for it correctly.* If your marriage failed, it's a sure sign that a part of you didn't want it after all. When you truly desire a relationship, you attract the right person and it works! That's so of all situations, but you need the effective skills. With the right spiritual tools, techniques, and instruction, you won't fail. Then, confidently, you can draw on your basic intuitive abilities to achieve your goals and transform your life into the wonderful, joyful, and fulfilling experience it was truly meant to be.

You can develop the talents necessary to create the life you want. Did you ever think that your stubborn streak would be a great asset to drawing what you want into your life? That ability to relentlessly pursue the perfect pizza in every restaurant in town or the unceasing and discriminating quest to get just the right shade of blue for your living room can and will, with a little education from this book, get you anything in the Universe that you desire.

Another talent in all of us that we might not be aware of or accustomed to using is our own psychic power. We all possess it. We're born with it. We tend to call it intuition or coincidence, like when you find you need advice from a particular person you trust who is far away and then out of the blue, she calls.

Not a coincidence at all. You psychically sent out a message to her psychic self in the form of a thought or desire. She picked it up on a subconscious level and woke up one day thinking to herself, "I've got to call Mary. I don't know why, but I do." We know why.

When these talents and abilities I'm speaking of are recognized and developed, they can give you the power to change your life. To help you to develop them, this book will give you practical tools, exercises, and rituals to use so that manifesting your needs and wants becomes easier and easier.

Getting what you want happens when you begin to use your talents and abilities to their greatest extent in making everyday decisions. I call this your psychic common sense. As you begin to use the part of your mind that is sensitive to thoughts and stimuli from everyone and everything on the Earth and beyond, you will become aware of the forces in the Universe that are there to help you. You do this every time you say a prayer. By calling on the unseen spiritual help available to all of us, you can be guided to your own success. When you begin to live each day from a limitless perspective—that is, accepting that anything you need or want can be yours—you will realize that nothing can stop you. This changes the way you think and the way you see the world. When your thinking changes, so does your life.

Every great athlete, performer, writer, artist, and business person has discovered that the way to make things happen lies beyond our physical selves. They've learned to work with their intuitive abilities to achieve their success. Over and over again we read about successful people who attribute their success to something greater than themselves, a power they didn't know they had, but when they acknowledged it, it became the source of their greatness. This power is also in you.

We tap into this power each day. For example, you're driving to work during rush hour and you get a "feeling" that you should not take your usual route, but an alternate route. Your logical mind is saying, "It'll take longer that way. I'll run into a lot of lights and I'll be late for work." Still, that feeling gnaws at you until you decide to take the alternate road. When you arrive at work you learn that there was a major accident on the road you usually take, a seven-car pileup. You think to yourself, "That could have been me. Good thing I took the other route. What a coincidence." Is it? I think not. It's your psychic common sense at work, and you listened to it. This is just one example, and there are countless others, of how our basic day-to-day decisions that we all have to make continually can be wiser, more perceptive, and get us more positive results.

We're very aware of these abilities in another area of our lives. Our dreams hold a fascination for many of us. I'm sure you've had dreams that were so vivid they felt absolutely real. Did you ever realize that your dreams are a part of your valuable psychic self? You can use the information in them to guide you to make important decisions and to help you get what you want.

A dear client of mine recently had a very important decision to make. It involved taking a new job, moving across the country, and uprooting her entire life. She asked for guidance before she went to sleep and, on waking the next morning, had her answer. In her dream her daughter, who lived in the area where she would be moving, told her everything would be fine, and she'd be happy making the move. She felt certain that this was direct guidance and relocated. Soon after, I received a letter from her telling me how happy she was that she had decided to listen to her dream. She keyed into her psychic common sense through her dream and allowed it to happen because, instinctively, she knew it was the right thing to do.

Many of my clients have told me that they have received similar guidance while in meditation. Our creative subconscious can form picture messages to help guide us. People report seeing a building or house, and then actually finding it. These are not unusual circumstances. When you realize that these things are probably happening in your life, too, you can use your psychic and intuitive power to give you the edge you need to make things happen.

There's no doubt that those of us who have the lives we want have learned how to make them happen and have tapped into this endless source of creativity. You can, too, as long as you take the necessary steps. So, first things first. Understand who you really are.

Take a Good Look at You

To get everything you want it's important to take a long, close look at you. How does your life measure up? Is it happy, fulfilling, abundant, prosperous, and loving? How do you feel when you take that look? If you're not happy with what you see, I suggest you shake up, wake up, and do it over. Create the life you've always dreamed about. Revolutionary new thinking, huh?

You've got to be ready to accept change into your life. We can get pretty lazy. Most of us are content to settle for the status quo because we're afraid of the future, of what we don't know. We resist committing to our future and the responsibility we share in shaping it. It's nice to think that the blessings of the Universe are somehow bestowed on us by a Greater Power, because it's easier than participating in their formation. It's also easier to blame God for not working these miracles in our lives, rather than accepting the part we play in making them happen. If you're one of those folks, I suggest you return this book to the store where you bought it and spend the money on aspirin instead, because I see lots of headaches ahead for you! But if you can and want to accept changes, like a life full of prosperity, love, good health, and happiness, then the answers to your questions are waiting and ready. They are locked in your soul, a part of the spirit that is you.

Flex Those Psychic Muscles

Here's an exercise to help you to assess who you really are. I've found in working with many people that it's best to keep a separate journal of your answers apart from this book, though writing in the spaces provided here is an option, too. That way you can follow your own progress and advancement just by glancing at your notes. Treat yourself to an attractive notebook that you dedicate only to your psychic-spiritual journey. Keep all your thoughts and experiences recorded as you move forward to getting those things that you want. You might want to organize your book so that you can leave a few pages blank after writing your answers to each exercise. Then you can go back and record your results days later, after putting the ideas into action. It is also very important to include your innermost feelings and thoughts as you move closer to your goals.

Exercise 1: Assessing Your Psychic-Spiritual Development

Answer the following questions as honestly as you can. Remember, you're trying to assess where you are right now in your psychic-spiritual development.

1. (This is the biggie, in my opinion.) Do you truly believe you can have everything you ever wanted in this lifetime? If so, why? If not, why?

2. Conjure up a genie, and make three wishes. If you could have what-ever you want, what are the first, second, and third most important wishes you would make? Now ask yourself why you picked these three.

_____

_____

_____

_____

_____

_____

_____

_____

_____

3. What emotional fears do you have that stop you from getting what you want? For example, are you afraid you aren't smart enough, good-looking enough, talented enough, or that you don't have enough money? You get the idea. List as many as you can think of.

_____

_____

_____

_____

_____

_____

_____

_____

_____

4. Are you willing to do your part and all you can to get what you want? What are you willing to do? (Take one desire you wish to manifest at a time, and list the things you're willing to do to get it. Remember to do this for all your wants and needs or, for right now, just the ones you're anxious to work on.)

When you've completed the questions, reread your answers to the first three. Can you see your own patterns? Are your fears stopping you? Does your disbelief in the possibilities of the Universe and your own ability get in your way?

Now take a look at your answer to question four, "Are you willing to do your part and all you can to get what you want? What are you willing to do?" If you had trouble answering it, you're holding onto the false notion that you have nothing to do with your future. Or you may not have been willing to invest as much time and energy as it will take to get you what you want. It's time to change, now.

If you had no trouble answering question four, get ready to move forward at warp speed, because you're well on your way to getting everything you ever wanted!

Questions, Questions, Questions

Of course there are questions running through your mind. Here are a few I hear often.

I do believe that I can have everything I ever wanted in this lifetime, but is belief enough?

Here's a resounding "yes." Belief is the most crucial key to success in manifesting your wants. And you don't even have to be that strong a believer either. That sounds strange but the Universe hears your intention the minute you put it in motion. All you have to do is believe it's possible that you can get it. That's it! That single glimmer of hope is enough to change your world. Even when you think you've lost hope or you act out of despair, you're actually not despairing at all because you're trying to find a way to make things happen for yourself. For instance, you may find yourself at a time in your life when you are severely depressed, and you think that you have to get help or you'll do yourself in. You ask a friend the name of her therapist and you make an appointment. You see, you're not really in despair—because if you were, you wouldn't be calling a shrink, your relatives would be calling an undertaker! That's my point. Part of you believes you can get better. This is belief in its truest and simplest form. And it's all anyone needs to accomplish great things.

What if I can't get over my fears? Will I still be able to have the life I want?

Eliminating fear is tough, but doable. It's not possible for us to eliminate all of our fears at once, but we can certainly get them under control so that they don't get in the way of achieving our goals. When we're in a fear state, our minds don't have room for anything else. Fear automatically eliminates hope and courage. Normal fears are everyday fare for most of us. They are our insecurities about having enough money to pay the bills, or whether or not our relationship will last. It's the abnormal fears that stop us. They can be deep-seated fears of inadequacy, success, or failure. Some of us are even afraid that we'll always be afraid! You'll need to delve into the reasons for your fears psychically and spiritually. The skills in this book will teach you a new way to face your fears, dissolve many of them, and control the rest.

What happens if I don't really know what I want?

Ah, this is a dilemma of infinite proportion! It's the age-old question arising all over again: "Why am I here?" It's very important to focus on what you want. If you don't know yet, the exercises in this book will help you to do this and decide upon your own unique needs and wants, and how to get them satisfied in this lifetime.

Now that you've got an idea of what is motivating you and who you are, as you approach your future, let's move ahead to identifying specific wants and needs.

Decide to Decide

There are times when the only really comfortable decision we are able to make is what to have for dinner. There are so many choices available to us in this day and age that life becomes overwhelming and options seem endless. That leaves most of us confused. We know there are goals we want to achieve in this lifetime—lotteries we'd like to win, places we'd like to go, people we'd like to attract into our lives—and yet it all seems untouchable. With so much out there, how can we truly know what we want?

Finding your focus in life may be the greatest challenge you've ever accepted. If you've said these words, "I'm going to find out why I came to this planet and I'm going to make it happen," then be happy with yourself, because you're one of those very special people who has recognized the part you play in creating your own future.

The power to have everything you ever wanted lies in your own hands, but first you must decide to go for it. You need *to decide* to decide to do it. Once that's done, the rest is a piece of cake.

Put yourself in league with the greats. Alexander Graham Bell decided to invent the telephone and Shakespeare decided to write plays. Michelangelo decided to paint a ceiling and Thomas Edison thought he'd shine a little light on everyone. What would life be like today if those people had stayed in their limbo of self-doubt and never decided to do their great work? We'd be isolated from each other, our lives would be devoid of great English poetry and Italian art, and we'd all be sitting in the dark!

It's Your Turn

The time has come for you to grab the reins and gallop forward. Decide to focus on the rest of your life and start right now. Take a look at the possibilities available to you. Assess what you can accomplish right now, not a month, a year, or ten years from now. Look to what you can make possible in this moment in time.

But you're saying, "What about long-term goals? Isn't it good to look ahead?" I'm not suggesting you walk around with blinders on, but I am suggesting that you begin now and not put off until tomorrow what you can do today. Don't get lazy and think that there's always tomorrow, because there are no guarantees. Before you know it, tomorrow is here and you're into regret and self-admonition for not going for it when you had the chance. Take it from me, if I hadn't told myself that time was of the essence, you wouldn't be reading this book today, because it would still be a figment of my imagination and my desire.

I can still hear you saying, "How? How do I get to the point where I decide what it is I want?" Here's how:

Look back on your life, so far, with love.

Know that you did the best you could, under the circumstances. Look at your past. Try to identify how you handled certain situations that didn't work out as you hoped. Decide what you could do differently, or better, if the situation happened again today. Now, mind you, I'm not telling you to try to change the past, but rather to use it as research in creating your future.

Forgive yourself and others for not getting everything you wanted or needed in the past.

That includes forgiving yourself first. Let go of the old you and say hello to the new you. Thank the old you for helping you get to this point, and send her on her way. It also means forgiving those people whom you might have blamed for your troubles, like your parents, unfaithful friends, children, lovers, ex-wives, ex-husbands, and so on. You get the idea. Know that they came into your life for a reason that is beyond the understanding of your conscious mind. They came, in their strange and sometimes painful way, to teach you and to help you grow spiritually into the wonderful person you deserve to be. They were gifts from God to help you get closer to your divine source. As the old saying goes, "God works in mysterious ways."

Don't be attached to the results.

This simply means that you shouldn't worry about how things will turn out. Know that no matter what happens, there is a divine plan in action. Trust in the power that is within you to lead you to the right place at the right time. You must trust that you will always get exactly what you should have for your spiritual growth, at this particular time in your life. I had always thought that I would have a life in the theater, and that's all I ever wanted. I tried to manifest acting and directing jobs and I got a lot of them. Then I had a very disappointing experience doing an off-Broadway show, and I asked the Universe to get me the perfect job—the one that would make me happy. Instead of Broadway, I founded a metaphysical center and church, which makes me happier than I ever thought possible—my dream job!

I know this story is hard to accept when you're on your last dime and the rent is due, but trust me, if you stop worrying about paying the rent, and start trusting that the opportunities are available to get it paid, they'll show up right in front of your nose!

Let's Get Physical

Yes, I know, all of this sounds good on paper, but how do we actually focus and decide? "Give me practical help," you say? I hear you, and here it is. The following exercise will help you put it all together in your mind, and discover what it is you really want.

Exercise 2: Assess Your Talents and Abilities

Looking at the following list of talents and abilities, choose the ones you believe you have within your own personality. You can write them in your journal or circle them here. Be honest and, most of all, be kind to yourself.

Patient	Enthusiastic	Outgoing
Warm	Happy	Creative
Spiritual	Artistic	Analytical
Good with children	Good with numbers	Good with hands
Good with people	Good with animals	Quick thinker
Good communicator	Tenacious	Strong
Loving	Wise	Good listener
Good with the Earth	Loyal	Honest
Assertive	Good achiever	Good at business
Psychic	Sensitive	Caring

Now put those talents and abilities in order of importance to you. What makes you feel good about yourself when you admit to it? What would you like to share with others? What do you do best, or what quality of your personality is strongest? Rate them from 1 to 5, 1 being the most important.

Looking at your assessment, what do you see? Do you want to share your art, handiwork, analytical skills, patience with others? What qualities can you use to help you to get the things you want in this life? Now choose to use them.

For instance, if you are a very patient, warm person who is good with numbers and you want a new, better paying job, can you see how you can use these qualities to get it? It takes time to get a new job, but if you're patient, that's no sweat for you. If you're warm, you can probably work on your interview skills to bring your natural warmth into meetings with potential employers. If you're good with numbers and you enjoy them, why not try thinking of employment in that area if you're not already doing it? You've got to pinpoint your abilities and massage them, so to speak, into a workable energy. Then that energy grows and gets bigger than you. And, before you know it, the vibrations are out there in the Universe and you're getting the things you always wanted.

But before you get too excited, there's more to do. Don't drop the book and run out into the world yet; I've got lots to tell you. Check out the next section. It'll help you to develop a new attitude, just in case your old one needs an overhaul.

Change Your Perspective

On New Year's Eve many of us declare our resolutions, and most of us will have broken that commitment by breakfast on New Year's Day. Why? Because we never actually believe we have what it takes to succeed. We expect some mysterious magical force will change us, and we'll be able to keep our promises to ourselves. The truth is, we have the power within us to make our dreams come true. All we need to do is change the way we think. It's that simple. Instead of expecting life to be a struggle, money to be scarce, and people to be difficult, work to be dull, *believe* you can change your life—and you will.

There's no mystery to it but, as a former teaching colleague of mine used to say, "You've gotta wanna." That's the key. Desire is the fastest route to the rest of your life. The spirit and enthusiasm that is part of the divine nature in all of us truly makes things happen. Change your thoughts and you change your world.

Each day we are given opportunities to create a new life. With every sunrise, the Universe gives us new possibilities, options, and people to help shape our future. It's what we do with these gifts and how we feel about them that determines the quality of our lives.

Seeing your life differently may be hard to master, but there's no in-between with this one. You change or you don't. That dictates your future.

Change is scary. To have everything you ever wanted, you need to change the way you see things, especially the way you see your life. We resist change in our lives. We resist committing to our future and the responsibility we share in shaping it. The power to live the life of our dreams and to draw all the things we need and want into our world comes from within our own consciousness. It is not outside of us. There is no energy acting upon us from some lofty place in the Universe. Our earthly, logical mind works together with the part of our consciousness that is God to shape the reality of our lives. The responsibility is ours and ours alone. If you want more from life, you need to do something about it. If you don't, no other force will do it for you.

Understanding your own creative power is essential to your success in getting what you want. Here are some insights to help you realize that you must change your attitude to accomplish your goals. Read them, understand that they are true, and absorb their messages.

Be optimistic.

Instead of being defeated by negative situations in your life, look for the lesson in them. Use the negative as a teacher and learn and move forward with a positive attitude.

Spread sunshine.

Smile a lot. Say nice things to people. Appreciate the love around you. Say, "Thank you."

Find the strengths hidden in your weaknesses.

For example, if you can see that being stubborn really hides within it tenacity, then you can begin to use your weaknesses as well as your strengths to create a new life.

Master these insights and you're on your way to a positive, loving, and spiritual reality. Then all you have to do is expect a miracle. And speaking of miracles—next, I'll help you to believe in them, and to accept that all things are possible.

Embrace Your Power

In my metaphysical practice, I've found that the hardest thing for people to do is to accept their greatness. Our mothers taught us as children not to be proud, conceited, or to toot our own horn, and frankly, we've taken these lessons a bit too far. It's one thing to let our ego get the better of us, but it's another thing to deny our divine greatness, our godliness within. We can recognize and accept that we have the power to make our dreams come true if we believe that we're part of a greater force or energy that can accomplish anything. If we truly understand that we are made of the same stuff as the Earth, trees, and stars, we can begin to see that the power to form our future lies within us.

Look around you. Accept your place in the Universe and know that you have all of it to support you in whatever you decide to do. That's connecting with your power; that's connecting with the Source that can help you achieve and attain everything you ever wanted. Make that connection and welcome the help that's so readily available to you. Accept your God-self and know that it is the part of you that can climb mountains!

It's not enough to accept the greatness of the Universe as the wind beneath your wings, so to speak, because there's more to do. You've got to accept you. Just as you are. It doesn't matter to the Universe if you're rich or poor, old or young, happy or sad, American or Chinese, Catholic or Pagan. The Universe relates to you as you, an individual source of power within a limitless energy field called life. In this sense we're all equal and no one gets special treatment. Know that anything can come to you as easily as it comes to one who might be considered fortunate. To the Universe, there are only those who choose to use their power and those who don't.

You've often heard of the rags to riches stories in Hollywood. A small-town kid makes good. Well, that's what I'm talking about. You don't have to start out advantaged to get what you want and need. You just have to know how to do it. Somehow, people like Dolly Parton, Garth Brooks, Anthony Robbins, and countless other poor kids who made it instinctively knew what I'm trying to tell you. And believe me, if they can do it, you can do it, too.

The key here is accepting who and what you are, right here, right now, and leading from your strengths. Recognize what you do well and what you don't do well. Embrace all of you. Say to yourself, "I'm okay. I can do some things really well, and other things I can improve on or get help with." When you admit this, you accept your humanness instead of feeling sorry for yourself, and then you can get moving.

A Question of Faith

But you say, "I'm riddled with self-doubt. I have no self-esteem, and I really can't do anything well. In fact, I haven't been able to do anything worthwhile my whole life. How can I ever get out of this miserable rut?" "Tsk, tsk, tsk," I say. Listen to yourself. Can you see how you are creating a self-fulfilling prophesy here? Sure, if you continue to reject yourself and your abilities, others will reject you too, and so will the Universe. That's the shocking truth. *The Universe will support, or give you back, whatever you put out to it.* So, if you put out self-doubt, low self-esteem, and self-hatred, you'll get more of it! That's what most people don't realize. They don't realize that the Universe/God is an essentially benevolent system that will give you whatever you seem to want. It doesn't judge what you send out into It, *It only responds or answers to it,* "thinking" that that's what you want to make you happy. Weird, but true. That's why it's so crucial to send out only positive messages, because then the Universe will support them and give you more positive things in your life. That's called a process. And a process never ends.

Do you ever notice that when you start out having a bad day, the rest of the day gets worse instead of better? That one negative incident in the morning, like the car not starting, begins a chain reaction for the rest of the day. The angrier or more annoyed you get as these situations happen, the faster they multiply. Nothing goes well and you can't wait to go to bed to get the day over with. In fact, if your day is really doomed, you'll have a mattress spring in your side all night!

I think you are beginning to see that what you set forth in motion within the Universe will definitely elicit a response. You must decide whether you want to send a positive or negative message. Whatever it is, you'll get so much of it back, it's amazing.

Doesn't it make sense to send out only positive messages, and then reap the benefits of unparalleled bliss? I think so, and so should you. Don't you think it's about time you accepted the possibility that you have the power to create anything?

There's hope for everyone. Accept who you are now. If you don't like what you see, change it, and know that the power to make the change is right at your fingertips. All it takes is having the right intention and a little patience.

Good Timing

We live in the now generation. Everything has to happen today, or better yet, yesterday. Time is always of the essence and we never seem to have enough of it. Maybe that's what we should be trying to manifest! Anyway, the question of how long things take is always on the mind of today's overextended and exhausted person. People often ask me, "So when will my intention actually happen in my life?" "How long do I have to do this until it works?" "How long does it usually take before you get what you want?" I hear you. I even feel anxious myself once in a while. When that happens I am reminded that all things take time. Some take less than others. My point is this: have patience. The Universe will give you what you want, but only when it is right and good for you to get it. It will come to you when it contributes to your spiritual growth or that of others. Now, this is not a cop-out. It's only the truth. You can't hurry the Universe.

Suppose you asked for love to come into your life, and you've got this idea of the perfect mate. Cute, smart, sensitive, strong, and rich. Okay—sounds good to me, too. Now just how easy is it to draw this wonderful person into your life? Do you think it's a small task or a great one? The intensity and difficulty of your request determines, in part, how long it takes to be answered.

Several years ago a dear friend and I talked about finding the perfect guy, as most single women do. She asked me how she could manifest him into her life. I asked her to be specific about the kind of man she wanted, what personality traits, etc. This was so she could begin sending positive thoughts out to the Universe. Since I am a minister, I blessed and consecrated a special candle for her that reinforced this intention to find the perfect love. She lit the candle and waited.

Two years went by. She was beginning to think it wasn't working. I told her that what she had asked for was a tall order and it would take time for the Universe to send her man into her life, so she sighed a big sigh and kept looking.

Finally, one day she called me with the good news—she had met him. He was all she'd asked for and more. She even realized why it took so long. The coincidences that brought them together were astonishing. Metaphysically speaking, there are no coincidences. It's all a matter of what's called synchronicity. This refers to events in the Universe that are somehow preplanned and all come together at the right time.

Anyway, my friend's synchronistic events were amazing. Her guy came from another country. She had to wait for the Universe to get him here to the U.S., into New York State, onto Long Island, into her town, and ultimately, into her neighborhood! Patience ruled the day.

Not all intentions take two years to manifest. Some happen the same day, within five, ten, or fifteen minutes of asking, in a day, a week, or a month. Remember, your request will be answered when the Universe/God feels it is in your highest and greatest good and in that of all those concerned. Divine will works in conjunction with your free will to make it happen.

In other words, you'll get what you want when all the factors are in place and all the pieces fit together within the span of energy that is your lifetime. Your dreams come true when all the factors involved arrive and come together at that particular moment, and no sooner.

This, of course, requires you to do something you may find difficult. Stop looking at time as getting away from you and as something that must be counted. Start looking at time as a series of events in your life that occur when all things are in the right order, when everything is in the right place at the right time.

A Friendly Word of Caution

Every single request you make of the Universe is *absolutely answered*. I'm not trying to scare you, but I am attempting to get you to accept responsibility for your actions. Manifesting using your psychic mind is very powerful. There are consequences to every situation, some positive, some not. In any case, you must be ready to receive your answer and to live and work with the results. As the old adage goes, "Be careful what you ask for, because you just might get it!" In this process of manifesting, you most surely will.

You've heard of people winning the lottery, a dream come true, and then losing it all. Money carries a certain obligation to use it wisely and manage it well. If the winner doesn't follow through on his part of the deal, he creates his own problems.

Be ready for all aspects of your request to enter your life, and be willing to take the good with the bad. Accept that, and you will surely build a positive, creative, abundant, and prosperous life, with a little help from the wizard within you.

Above All, Say Thanks

Gratitude is the final concept you must understand if you want to create a life of fulfilled hopes, dreams, and desires. No matter what happens, we must be thankful to God/the Universe/Spirit, the Greater Power, or whatever you call It, for even listening to us in the first place. Start out every request, intention, or prayer with gratitude, and everything you need, want, and desire will already be yours.

CHAPTER 2

Karma, Reincarnation, and Lessons

*E*ven though you're anxious to begin manifesting what you want, you still need to understand why we do what we do in this lifetime, or any other, for that matter. Why do we want what we want? Why do we make the choices we make?

We've come to this life with a guiding set of principles and a suitcase full of lessons we have yet to learn. The fact is that we packed the bag ourselves. In each lifetime that we have lived, we have learned some of our Earth-school lessons and not others. Those we haven't learned we pack in our karma suitcase to be carried over to our next lifetime. When we get here, we unpack the bag and wear the lesson-clothing until it serves its purpose and we are done with it. So you see, we arrived from Spirit, karma suitcase in hand, ready to travel through this Earth stopover on our way to a place called Enlightenment.

Every day, we meet the consequences of our previous deeds and attitudes in this lifetime. So, too, can we meet the consequences of previous deeds and attitudes from another lifetime.

Get it? *What you reap, you sow.* So, we need to be careful about the kind of seeds we plant. I prefer roses to weeds, myself.

Next Stop: Karma Mountain

I use this corny image to drive home my point—that living this lifetime can sometimes feel like climbing a mountain. Karma is not something that dooms us to spend our lives endlessly searching for fulfillment; rather, karma is a gift from the Universe. It is designed to help us learn our lessons and spiritually grow. Karma is the pop quiz of the cosmos. If we pass each test, we move on to bigger and better things. If we fail, we simply have to repeat the lessons. And so it goes.

Now, you may be wondering, "What exactly is karma?" Maybe it'll be more helpful to tell you what it is not. It is not cosmic payback. We haven't come back here to make up for some nasty thing we did in another lifetime. The ominous concept of "pay now or you'll pay later" has scared us all to death. We seem to feel that life is constantly paying us back for some unknown wrong we committed. How depressing. An amazing number of people carry that burden around for life. It's time we let it go.

Here is a way to understand karma. For example, you might think that your lover left you because you left him in another lifetime, and now you're getting your comeuppance. Well, that's not necessarily the case. You're really dealing with a greater spiritual issue here, and your lover is a sort of instrument for your learning, the bow that helps you play the violin. You have most likely shared other lifetimes with him and you have become each other's teachers here on Earth. The greater issue could be that your spirit wanted to learn about how it feels to be rejected or abandoned by someone you love. Your lover would most likely have similar related issues, like wanting to learn what it is like to break someone's heart or be the source of someone's pain. This seems strange, but remember, we came to learn about even the dark side of human nature.

Another example of karma is victimization in some form. You may be the victim of some violent crime. It doesn't necessarily mean that you were once violent against your attacker in another lifetime. It means that your two souls came together because you had related issues to resolve, related lessons to learn, and each of you enabled the other to learn them. You both had parts to play in the scenario, based on the life plans you created when you were both in spirit form.

Karma is not always negative, you know. The whole idea of living a spiritual life and moving to our individual divine greatness is to create and enjoy positive events and people in this lifetime, too. An example of good karma—and there are many, I might add—is a positive, loving relationship. In contrast to the previous example of lovers causing each other pain, there are clearly relationships that seem to be made in heaven. You know the kind—two people born to be together. This is a clear indication of a loving relationship so deep and fulfilling that its energy is carried forward into another lifetime. These two souls are so close and devoted they continue to incarnate together, lifetime after lifetime, to experience the unconditional love and joy they have for one another. Interestingly, many of these souls reincarnate over and over again as lovers. They have been commonly dubbed soulmates.

Positive karma can also be seen in close, supporting friendships and families. Many times a soul with a specific mission reincarnates with other compatible souls in order to accomplish that mission. How far would Jesus Christ have gotten without the love and support of Mary and Joseph, his Earth parents? Really good karma there, I'd say!

If you feel blessed and happy with your life most of the time (barring the occasional trauma or two), if people are kind to you and helpful, if others love and respect you, then it's safe to say you have created some pretty wonderful karma.

Just as you and other folks have come to learn painful lessons, you have also reincarnated to learn joyful ones. Hopefully, the latter outnumber the former. Anyway, you can unpack happiness from that karma suitcase, as well.

In the ancient language of Sanskrit, *karma* literally means "work, deed, or act," which can also be translated as "cause and effect." In each lifetime, we create thought and action. If the thoughts or acts are good ones, they set up a psychic chain reaction that will eventually return to you as good in your life. In other words, whatever you cause to happen can have an effect on your current lifetime, or those lifetimes to come. Therefore, if you choose to have positive, loving thoughts and actions, or create positive causes, you will see the effects in your future as positive events or relationships.

To further understand this crazy thing called karma, you've got to realize that karma is one of the reasons we came here, the embodiment of our Earth-school curriculum, the syllabus of our life. If we had no karma, good or bad, we'd have no reason to reincarnate.

In your first incarnation, you began to create karma. Karma, added to your experiences of all your past lifetimes, makes you who you are today. Your uniqueness comes from this precise combination of energies that only you possess. You are one of a kind. You came to this spiritual point in your existence and your soul developed to this extent based upon all the learning you've done in the past. You'll be a totally different person after each lesson is learned.

In order to get everything we've ever wanted, we also need to know how to eliminate the blocks that might be subconsciously sabotaging us. We need to know what, if anything, stands in our way or prevents us from attaining our desires. Sometimes karma from another lifetime that is negative and has not been resolved is the block. If we analyze and understand the events from another lifetime that have created the block, we can release it. Then we are able to attract what we truly want into our lives. It's good, sound psychic common sense.

Just think about how much you've learned already in this lifetime alone. Imagine now that this knowledge is combined with all the knowledge of your previous incarnations—everything that you ever learned. It's astounding! *You* are astounding. And you have much to continue to learn and give to the world.

Here I Am—Again; Or, the Big Plan Fulfilled

When a soul enters a new body after physical death, it is said to be reincarnated or born again. Metaphysicians believe that we have lived many lifetimes. They believe that we have the option to choose to be born again. This depends upon the karma we left behind and our desire to resolve it. So, if we come back to Earth in another time, in another body, we do so with a plan to get rid of the blocks, or negative karma we have created in other lifetimes, enjoy the happy results of the good karma, make a contribution to humankind, to learn new lessons, and above all, to serve Spirit.

Contrary to common thought, we do have control. By now you're thinking, "Sure I do. If I have so much control, why am I so miserable?" Well, that has to do with *how* and *whether* you've learned your lessons. I'll get to that later. For now, it's important to accept the part you play in the creation of your life. It all relates directly to reincarnation.

Before we take the slow boat to this planet, we have the privilege, while in spirit form, to choose our next "big plan." We choose our new lessons to be learned, we make a deal with other souls to help us, and we agree to help them. Then we decide what point in time, or what century, we want to experience. We choose our gender, race, nationality, hair color, eye color, weight, height, everything, all designed to help us achieve what is called our life purpose, the work we wish to do to benefit humankind. This is not a free ride. God gives us the privilege of coming here and, in return, we give back to others in the form of our life purpose. What that purpose is and how we fulfill it is strictly up to our free will. *It's all up to us.* God gives us the go-ahead, we wait for the souls who have agreed to be our parents to get here first, then we make the grand entrance, kicking and screaming (it takes guts to leave bliss and come back here, you know), and the whole thing begins.

I could write an entire book on life purpose alone, but let it suffice for now to say that honoring our Creator, serving others, and learning our spiritual lessons are what it all boils down to. How we choose to do that is subject to the divine gift of ultimate choice, or free will.

That Free Will Thing

It's hard to understand that we actually have choices in the creation of our lives, because it's so much easier to depend on some outside force to take care of us. That leaves us blameless if we make some foolish decisions. Remember comedian Flip Wilson's statement: "The devil made me do it!"

Yes, it is true that we and God have planned the whole thing before we came here, but we did not plan our precise words, thoughts, and decisions. These details are up to us. We can fulfill our plan and reach our spiritual goal any way we want. The goal remains the same, even though there are many different paths to it. Our object is to get from point A, birth, to point B, spiritual enlightenment, and we have countless options, choices, and decisions available to us while we walk our path on the Earth. In the end, it's our choice how we travel to our spiritual destination or live our life.

If part of our plan is to learn our lessons with a partner in this lifetime, we will. So, even if it seems we're never going to meet Mr. or Ms. Right, it doesn't mean we won't. It's just taking some time to happen because we made certain choices along the way that could have taken us off the direct route to each other. We might have each married, gotten divorced to resolve karma with someone else, and are now spiritually ready to meet.

We must wait until the time is right for everything. But this book is about how we can make sure that we make the right choices to get what we want and need, and to fulfill our plan. These are the desires and intentions we ask of the Universe.

The ability to get the things we want is our gift from the Universe to help make our spiritual journey fun. We use our free will and psychic common sense to draw our heart's desires to us. Learning how to master and use these talents ensures that we enjoy the ride.

Learn Your Lessons Well

The great American writer and humorist, Mark Twain, shared a thought about learning that I'd like to include here. It's from *Following the Equator*, which he wrote in 1897. It's still so relevant today:

> We should be careful to get out of an experience only the wisdom that is in it—and stop there; lest we be like the cat that sits down on a hot stove-lid again—and that is well; but also she will never sit down on a cold one anymore.

Twain tells us to learn, let the pain go, and move on, but also to proceed with caution. We come here to resolve karma, create new karma, and serve God and other people. But, most importantly, we come here to learn to do it better, to make life a joyful experience for ourselves and others. Learning from the past and making wise choices are the keys.

"So, just what are these lessons?" you say. I mentioned earlier that this life on Earth is just one big classroom. When we are born we enter the classroom of our choice, based on the course we want to take. I remember registering for classes as an undergraduate in college and finding the ones I wanted were full and I couldn't get in. The classes here on Earth are never full, so we get to take all the courses we want. We've chosen those particular courses when we put our life-plan together between incarnations. Our karma helps us determine what we want to learn and experience when we come back. We then begin to attract the right circumstances and people that help us fulfill our plan. They are our teachers and textbooks, so to speak. When considering karma it is important to understand the following:

- The karma we brought back with us is a combination of positive and negative lessons we still need or want to learn.

- Karma is the unfinished business we returned to resolve.

- Lessons are the opportunities available that enable us to resolve our karma.

There is another important aspect to this concept of learning our lessons. Since we have created our original plan it follows, according to metaphysical philosophy, that we also create our lessons and the circumstances within which they occur. *We mastermind the whole thing.* When situations appear to be negative it is hard to understand why we would give ourselves such grief. Yet we do.

Angrily, many of my students, clients, and church members ask questions like those that might be crossing your mind right now, such as, "Why would I create this car accident that left me with permanent damage to my back and constant pain?" or "Why would I create such an abusive marriage?" A paralyzed college student of mine with severe muscular dystrophy nearly broke my heart when he imploringly looked into my eyes and said, "Then you're saying I wanted to be like this, and that I created my disability." I took a deep breath, gulped, and said, "Yes."

As outrageous as it may sound, we do design our own lessons. We don't create them in the sense that we consciously want to have physical or emotional hardship. Rather, we create the overall lesson to be learned first, while we are in spirit form, as part of our plan. Then, we come to Earth with the physical body necessary to assist us in learning our lessons. Hence, my disabled student, before he was ever born, decided he needed an afflicted, handicapped body in order for his spirit to grow, to make his contribution to humankind and, most importantly, to truly know his God. He understands this better than anyone I've ever known. Today he is an aspiring television screenwriter, penning deeply inspirational and touching stories about what it means to live with a debilitating disease. I'm sure millions of viewers will benefit from his work. This is a truly noble existence with a tremendous karmic lesson.

As to why we would create a car accident or abusive marriage, the reason is the same. We do it subconsciously, to set up circumstances in which to fulfill our life purpose. The sooner we learn, the faster we grow. Then the lessons become easier and easier and fewer and fewer in number until the only karma we are working through is the positive, loving kind. That's when we know we're getting closer to our spiritual goal or enlightenment.

Human beings tend to focus on the negative lessons and gloss over the positive ones, perhaps because they don't seem as dramatic or earth shattering. We perceive most situations with the attitude, "Now what?" and live our lives waiting for something to go wrong, particularly when everything is going well. We are weird. How often do we appreciate or even recognize how well off we are? Learning does not have to be painful. Your third-grade teacher, if she was anything like mine, Sister Mary Frightening, has terrified you into believing school is hell. It's not. It can actually be heaven.

I use an example in my classes to help students understand this negative focus and how it can stop us from enjoying the lessons. Let's say you and a dear friend meet for lunch. She tells you how great you look and goes on and on about your beautiful blouse, how the color really enhances your eyes, how thin you've gotten and how that skirt takes another ten pounds off of your already slim frame but you could have made a better choice with the shoes. The coat you're wearing is fabulous and your overall look, she says, "makes Cindy Crawford look homely."

Which, of all these statements, do you remember? What stays with you? Not how gorgeous you look, but rather your knee-jerk reaction is, "What's wrong with my shoes?" My students fall for it every time. We laugh realizing that the single negative comment is the one we can't shake from our minds. It's the same with our lessons. The negative or difficult ones take over our consciousness. That's why it seems like there are more of them than the positive ones.

A consequence of our lessons is that they are destined to be repeated until we learn them. If you wear the ugly shoes when out with another outspoken friend, your feelings may be hurt again, only now it's worse, because two people think you have bad taste! What's the lesson? Don't wear those shoes if you can't take the feedback? No, the real lesson has to do with your self-esteem and how you handle criticism.

I wish all our lessons were this obvious. Unfortunately, they are much more subtle and require us to think, meditate, and come to an often painful conclusion. But that's the stuff we came to experience—the thinking, the learning, and the growing. Once the lesson is understood it's over. We don't have to learn it again, therefore we will not attract a similar situation in the future. That's the good news.

Our object here on Earth is to accept our lessons, both simple and profound, and decipher what we are trying to learn. We figure out our lessons through introspection, accepting our responsibility within the situation, and turning over what we don't understand to the Universe. This means we have faith. We reason that there are some lessons we'll never figure out, but that they are necessary for our spiritual growth, and in so doing we learn. So you see, we can learn and resolve certain karmic lessons by simply realizing that we can't figure them out. The wisdom is hidden in some lessons, but nevertheless we gain from them. They are simply meant to teach us to believe and trust in the Greater Source that created us. Other lessons help us to make changes in our lives so that we don't have the same situation happen again. Ergo, the power is back in our own hands. That is the basic truth of the whole learning process.

I wish I could tell you how to eliminate your painful lessons so you could just sail through this lifetime happily. But without our lessons we'd have no growth. Our lives would be stagnant and boring. "I'll take a little boring from time to time," you're thinking. Look at it this way—without your lessons of pain, how would you know joy? Without joy, how would you understand sadness? We would all be walking around like zombies, an entire world of robots, like *Star Trek's* Mr. Spock, Vulcans without feelings, attitudes, or the ability to know love. See why lessons are so important to our very existence? They teach us to become loving, caring, happy, and productive human beings. How do you like that karma?

In the process of becoming this wonderful person, the people and circumstances appear in our lives that create the environment within which we learn.

We have accidents, toothaches, car trouble, and bad dates. We have parties, celebrations, triumphs, and profound spiritual experiences. We get hired, fired, married, divorced, give birth, mourn death, and on and on it goes. All of it is meant to happen so that our spirit, our soul, will find its way back home. In other words, we learn through the good and the bad what it means to be human, and what a gift life is. In short, we begin to understand God.

The lessons we are here to learn are as different and varied as we are. Everyone has his own unique plan of study. You will have no problem getting everything you ever wanted as long as you use your psychic common sense and know what you don't want. Accepting your lessons and determining the reasons behind them gives you your power. When you are empowered by your knowledge and experience, you can figure out what your true intentions are, what you truly want and need, and then you can manifest it.

You have a special relationship with your karma that is unique. This next exercise is an opportunity for you to think about your lessons and karma, and the people and events that affect your life.

As always, record your answers in your journal (or here, in the spaces provided), so you can track your progress.

Exercise 3: You and Your Karma, Part I—Self-Analysis

Ask yourself the following questions and record your answers:

1. If you unpacked your karma suitcase today, what would you find?

A. List the most significant events.

_____

_____

_____

_____

_____

_____

_____

_____

B. List the people who have been the most important to you.

_____

_____

_____

_____

_____

_____

_____

_____

_____

2. What negative lessons do you feel you've unpacked and resolved from your karma suitcase?

_____

_____

_____

_____

_____

_____

_____

_____

_____

A. Make a list of past and current painful events of your lifetime. This could drag up some very uncomfortable feelings, but it's a necessary part of your growth process, so give it a shot.

_____

_____

_____

_____

_____

_____

_____

_____

B. List the emotions that were hardest to cope with surrounding these events.

_____

_____

_____

_____

_____

_____

_____

_____

_____

3. What happiness have you unpacked from your karma suitcase?

_____

_____

_____

_____

_____

_____

_____

_____

_____

4. List the most joyful moments of your life (have fun with this!).

_____

_____

_____

_____

_____

_____

_____

_____

_____

_____

_____

Exercise 3: You and Your Karma, Part II— Relationship Analysis

Try this next part by considering someone who is very important in your life. It could be a spouse, lover, best friend, or parent (you might want to try it for each one of these people), then answer the following:

1. Overall, is your relationship with this person positive or negative?

_____

_____

_____

_____

_____

_____

_____

_____

_____

2. What positive or negative lessons are the two of you sharing?

_____

_____

_____

_____

_____

_____

_____

_____

3. What are you teaching each other?

_____

_____

_____

_____

_____

_____

_____

_____

4. What lessons have you already learned and are continuing to learn together?

_____

_____

_____

_____

_____

_____

_____

_____

_____

_____

It's only fair to tell you that in some relationships you might not know the full extent of your karma for years, yet you are teaching each other each day your relationship exists, so you continue to create karma together. At the very least, you can objectively recognize whether it's good or bad from the way you get along.

It's All in the Past

Recognizing the various karmic relationships you have in this lifetime is a very powerful key to manifesting. Studying our past lives and how they impact this life is extremely useful. We can then use this knowledge from karmic experiences and past lives to help us attain our goals in this current lifetime.

In my private practice my clients have been able to overcome chronic problems such as serious illness, emotional trauma, and even obesity armed with the knowledge of their past lives. I've done many past life regression hypnosis sessions where clients are able to access the past lives that are hidden within their subconscious minds. Under hypnotic suggestion a person may move back in time to the situation that began a particular karma they are trying to resolve now. One of my clients witnessed a lifetime in which she died of starvation. Knowing this and recognizing that she is not the victim in this lifetime helped her to release her fears and stop overeating, resulting in a tremendous weight loss.

Not all of us need to undergo hypnosis to understand our karma and how we can improve our lives just by recognizing it. We simply need to believe that every circumstance of our lives happens for a reason and that this reason embodies our karmic lessons. Then we make a commitment to ourselves to release the hold these past problems have on us. We can do this even if we're not exactly sure what that hold is. We must simply trust that we can overcome anything destructive that is hidden in our subconscious mind. That is all. In accepting that, events begin to flow through your life with less trouble and strife.

I hope you've learned some interesting things about yourself and your destiny. Just thinking about such things helps open your channel to whatever you want in this lifetime. Remember, *positive thoughts create positive results.* And speaking of opening that vast remarkable treasure that is your mind, the next chapter will help you prepare your psychic-intuitive self. It is this part of our being that enables us to draw upon all of the energy in the Universe, no holds barred. Developing these skills sends powerful vibrations into the Universe and literally enables us to create anything we want. And guess what? Anyone can do it.

PART TWO

How You Do It

CHAPTER 3

Your Psychic Tune-Up

*A*t the start of this book, I told you that getting what you want happens when you begin to use what I call our psychic common sense. "Just what is this ability?" you ask. Well, it is a simple idea, really. Basically, psychic ability is rooted in your subconscious mind. Allow me to illustrate.

Just for a moment, have some fun and visualize with me. Imagine that your brain is a library building. See a beautiful building in your mind's eye, a majestic Gothic structure full of wisdom. The main entry door you see looming before you is open. You have easy access to the main floor of the library. This, if you will, is your conscious mind, the waking state of all of us. Now, as you walk through the main floor of the library, you are free to read any book you want. You are totally aware. But you see a sign that says, "Second floor locked—no entry." You wonder why you can't get to the wisdom on the second floor. Where's the key? Why is it closed off? It's there, you know that, but yet you can't reach it.

The second floor is your subconscious mind. The "books" stored up there have never been read by your conscious mind. But they still exist, even if you never see them. Now, imagine that you could find the key to open the second floor of the library of your brain, and freely read all the books there. You would gain infinite knowledge, power, and the ability to make anything happen in your life, because all the knowledge you need is stored there waiting to be read. What I'm saying is that using the basic psychic-intuitive ability we all possess is the key to unlocking the door to our subconscious mind and to achieving anything we desire.

Hey, You, Get Your Head in the Clouds!

The great psychologist Carl Jung, in his countless writings, has told us that there exists a part of the human mind he called the collective unconscious. Jung said that it is an energy that all humans share. Now, let me explain in plain English.

In simple terms, the collective unconscious is that basic part of our subconscious mind that is like every other human's. You know, it's like having two arms, a nose, and two feet. It's a part of our mind that we all have in common. The astounding thing here is that it's not just ours, like my consciousness or your consciousness. Jung tells us that while we do have an individual conscious mind, we are somehow connected to every other human's brain as well, as though we are all part of the same mind.

To understand this concept, envision a huge white billowing cloud of energy. Now imagine that every human being, alive or not, is floating on that cloud. As we all sit there and float together, we share that common space. We are part of the energy of that cloud. Now imagine that a part of that cloud breaks away from the main. One of us is floating on that smaller piece for a while, and then, when our adventure is through, we drift back to that main cloud that was, and is, our true home.

We all knew each other when we lived on that cloud and we never forget our bond even if we drift apart. We share common knowledge. We share a common wisdom. Our minds share a common origin. That is the collective unconscious. It's unconscious because we are not necessarily aware of this bond and because the information stored there is so vast that if we had total conscious recollection, we'd blow up our limited little brains. So you see, the knowledge and wisdom of the Universe is all really there for all of us to tap into.

This is the principle behind a psychic reading. A psychic can get to this information, this "cloud," because he or she is like a radio receiver that can pick up many frequencies or channels. Each person's mind has this sensitivity to a degree, depending upon his or her need for it in this lifetime. Some of us are meant to help others with this ability, as I am, and therefore it is developed to a greater degree. Others of us, who are not the seers and prophets of the planet, have a more limited psychic capacity, but we all have it. That's the message. The good news is that we just need to simply learn about how to use it, and decide to use it, and we'll have as much as we and our divine source have planned for us to have in this lifetime.

I guess the operative phrase here is "use it or lose it"! Don't let your psychic common sense go to waste because of fear or laziness. Yes, it is true that for some of us this ability came easily, but for most it is something to develop, study, and perfect. In my practice, my function has been to teach others how to use their psychic common sense. Countless lives have been changed in the process. Many of my students have come to know that life can be all we want it to be, and more.

Knowing yourself and how you perceive life is very important to your basic psychic preparation. Here's an exercise to help you get started accepting yourself and your power to move mountains—well, the mountain that is your life, at least.

This exercise will help you to look at yourself objectively, and at the way you handle day-to-day living. It is based upon Jung's personality inventory, with a few major adjustments. It will tell you if you're facing life in a positive or negative way. You might be surprised to know that you handle life in a negative fashion—no wonder the laundry never gets done, the kids don't do well in school, and you never have enough money to pay your bills. Here, see for yourself.

Let's Get Started

Circle the letter or the response you feel best describes your attitude and the way you live your life today. You can record these in your journal, if you like, and leave a space for your comments.

Exercise 4: Personality Inventory

1. When my opinions vary from those in my circle, I am most often:

    a. intrigued   b. uncomfortable

2. When getting ready to travel, I usually pack up:

    a. at leisure, in advance   b. at the last moment

3. Assuming I was equally familiar with both plays, I would prefer to go to the theatre to see:

    a. Romeo and Juliet   b. Hamlet

4. When confronted with misfortune, it is my more frequent impulse to:

    a. search for the causes   b. feel defeated.

5. When it comes to dealing with practical life details, I tend to be:

    a. skillful   b. impatient with them

6. Once I choose a goal:

    a. I carry it through   b. I have trouble accomplishing it

7. When I find myself being neat and orderly it feels like:

    a. something inborn   b. a real achievement

8. I:

    a. think more about the future than the past

    b. think more about the past than the future

9. In making decisions, I:

    a. generally trust my intuition

    b. generally trust physical facts

10. When facing a decision that will change my life significantly, I most often:

    a. collect my thoughts and decide quickly

    b. am slow to decide and put it off

Scoring:

Now add up the number of "a's" and the number of "b's" you circled, separately.

If you answered 6–10 questions with "a" answers, you're already looking at life fairly positively. It should be easy to accept your own power and begin manifesting.

If you answered 6–10 questions with "b" answers, you're perceiving life negatively, and are not sending the right messages out into the Universe. Things need to change before you can successfully begin manifesting.

If you answered 5 "a" and 5 "b" responses, you're hanging in the balance. You need to make some minor adjustments in your thinking so that you tip the scales to the more positive side. Try eliminating the words "never" and "can't" from your vocabulary. That works wonders immediately.

Overall, there is hope for everyone. This exercise is just meant to give you an objective look at your own patterns of thinking. Accept who you are now. If you don't like what you see, change it, and know that the power to make the change is right at your fingertips. All it takes is having the right intention. The following psychic power tools will show you how to change your life and start a more positive way of thinking, using the power that is already within you. That's the power, through pure thought and intention, that will get you everything you ever wanted. Embrace it now!

Psychic Power Tools

Okay, just what are these psychic tools? There's nothing spooky about them. They are merely powers of the mind and spirit, ways to use a portion of the brain's ability that most people are unaware of or are too afraid to use. I can tell you that if you give them a try, you'll be amazed at the results. Yes, I'm asking you to throw away conventional, logical thinking and rely on the part of your mind that is creative and full of images and adventures. Accept the challenge, believe that these talents can help you, and you're on your way to happiness.

The following is a list of these tools that I've found to be the most effective in our quest to create the life we want. I'll explain each of them later on, but for now, you should know what you're in for and what challenge you've accepted by just reading this book!

Psychic Power Tool 1: Proper Breathing

Learning to breathe may seem silly but in fact, with each calculated deep breath, we wash away tension, stress, and all of the junk in our conscious mind. This clears the way for powerful thoughts that can change our reality.

Psychic Power Tool 2: Meditation

This is your greatest tool to getting everything you ever wanted. When you meditate you literally lighten your physical body's energy vibration and, believe it or not, you can tap in directly to the information stored in your sub-conscious mind! It's true. You can get there from here!

Psychic Power Tool 3: Visualization

The power of our minds to "see" pictures can draw that very picture to us. In other words, what we can envision, we can have. It's a very powerful ability, and so easy to master. What you see is definitely what you get!

Psychic Power Tool 4: Intuition

Your intuition is the vehicle that drives you forward, the Mercedes-Benz of your psychic mind. It helps you clearly see the situation before you by taking you in one direction or another, and it helps you make appropriate decisions. Getting everything you ever wanted greatly depends upon listening to the intuitive voice inside you, and then acting on it.

Putting all these tools to work for you makes perfect psychic common sense. Tune up your tools, keep them in working order, care for them and use them, and you'll have at your fingertips the skills you need to create the life you want.

Sharpening Your Psychic Power Tools

It's not enough to recognize and accept these skills. You've got to sharpen and hone them. How? To use your psychic common sense, you need your logical mind to take a back seat to your intuition. That's very difficult for most folks. In fact, in my teaching, I find myself telling people over and over again not to look at their lives strictly from a logical perspective, because Spirit works in illogical ways.

For instance, you might want a new job, and you think that looking in the newspaper want ads, seeing a headhunter, and networking are the logical ways to get it. I'm suggesting that your mind is so powerful that you can get your job using that power. I know a man, one of my longtime clients, who made it happen.

This man badly wanted a new job. He began to meditate and created a picture in his mind of the job he wanted. He listened to the messages his intuition was sending, followed his gut feelings when making decisions, and in a matter of two months he had his dream job. He did all those logical things, too, to keep the energy in motion, but the job came by what we might call a fluke. A former customer at his current job remembered him years later and was inspired to call him out of the blue because he had an opening that he felt was perfect for him. The customer didn't even know he was looking for a new job. And there it was, absolutely not logical, but obviously possible. His powerful mind sent a clear message and someone's radio receiver picked it up! Start sending your own messages and see what happens.

When I was describing this technique to my dear friend Sara, she was fighting me with her logic, even though she truly believes anything is possible. This is true for most of us because we in our Western society are conditioned from birth to plod along in this life, step by step. It's hard to change our thinking, skip a few of those steps, and go straight to the Source. When you do, you use those tools I'm telling you about. In our conversation, Sara's resistance led me to say something that made sense to her. "Lighten up the logic and tune up the intuitive!"

Now, speaking of tuning up, let's take a look at each one of the psychic power tools and how you can use them to turn on your radio receiver to the big broadcasting channel in the sky.

Tools of the Trade

Psychic power tools are a sure-fire way for you to begin to create all that you wish to have in this lifetime. The secret here, my friends, is commitment. I call it the "C word" because so many people are afraid of it. Like anything else, you must realize that your attention, dedication, perseverance, and patience will be needed when you begin to tap into your spiritual self and make things happen in your life.

The following tools are the step-by-step instruments used for manifesting. You'll need to master them if you're serious, and not leave any out, each time you attempt to receive something from the Universe. Once you become an old hand at it, the process gets easier. I remember when I first learned to drive at sixteen. I thought I'd never be able to remember all the things I had to do to get the car moving, and now I don't even think about it. It has become second nature. That's what will happen when you get used to asking for help this way, too. It becomes so natural that you'll be able to leave this book home and manifest anywhere, anytime.

I think you understand the importance of following a regime in order to condition your mind so that it becomes a natural response. Let's get going.

Psychic Power Tool 1: Proper Breathing

With each breath you take, you renew your body and quiet your mind. When you deliberately breathe deeply you send a message to your body to slow down. From a spiritual perspective, the breath is considered a cleansing that washes away any residue that may cloud your mind, such as tension, stress, worries, and any uncomfortable emotions like anger and fear. Breathing opens your mind to higher levels of understanding. It actually slows down your physical body processes and prepares you to focus on your abilities beyond the physical. It gets you ready to change your reality with your thoughts. Here's how to do it:

Exercise 5: In with the Good Air . . .

Do this breathing exercise when you are alone and won't be disturbed. Turn off the lights and the phone, put the cat out, and just get ready to relax.

1. Sit comfortably in a chair, feet flat on the floor. Put your hands on your lap, palms up. Be sure not to use a chair with arms, or remove your arms from the chair just to prevent your arms from falling asleep. That could jolt you right out of your calm state.

2. Close your eyes and shift your conscious focus to your breathing. Notice how your body responds to each breath. Feel how your chest rises and falls and peacefully observe this soothing process for a moment, as you allow yourself to gently calm down and relax. Just keep focusing on what this breathing process feels like, and nothing else. Notice everything about it, and especially how calm it makes you. Do this for a few moments.

3. Now we're going to shift into our cleansing breath. We'll do three cleansing breaths, inhaling through the nose, and exhaling through the mouth. It's important to breathe very deeply on the inhalation, and even if you make noise, that's okay. Feeling silly is a sure sign that you're doing it right. On the exhale, be sure to let all the air out fully through the mouth, even if you feel as though you're blowing it out, and make some noise when you do this, too. Then you'll be assured you're not holding anything back. Remember, this is a purging of sorts, and it's meant to clear out your system. So just take in that new fresh air and blow out all that old junk. Do this three times, slowly. As you take each breath, focus your mind on how it feels to take air in and let it out. Just concentrate on the process, and let all other thoughts drift away.

Now don't you feel better, more relaxed, and calm? You can do this anywhere, anytime, even if you're not trying to manifest anything. It's a great stress reliever, and it's free! By releasing through breathing, you've begun to prepare yourself for the entire manifesting process.

You need to do this for each request you have. Remember, it's important to go through all the steps every time you set out to create what you want.

After you've slowed down your body and mind through this rhythmic breathing, the next natural step is to go deeper into the recesses of your mind through meditation, the second psychic power tool.

Psychic Power Tool 2: Meditation

Meditation takes you even further toward your goals. The ancients used it as a form of prayer, relaxation, and healing. It is said that the great masters of Tibet can stop the beating of their hearts in meditation. It's quite powerful. For our purposes, no heart-stopping will be necessary. All we need to do is slow down our physical body's energy vibration. This will happen naturally. When you have achieved a state of deep meditation, you unlock the door to your subconscious mind. That is where your power to create the life you desire lies.

When you change your subconscious tapes, you change your life. When you tell your subconscious mind to do something, it does. We're going to reprogram it to get you what you want in place of the tape that says, "Good stuff is for other people," or "I'll never get what I want." When your subconscious replaces doubt with the concept of unlimited power, it naturally filters into your conscious mind and you start to feel that getting what you want is really possible! Then an even greater thing happens: you start attracting all that you need to make what you want a reality. Doors open, people who can help come into your life, and things start to develop. You see, if you change your mind, you change your life.

That's what we're aiming for here. Meditation is the greatest tool to getting all you want or need. It's in the meditative state that we begin manifesting. So now, let's take a look at a simple meditation that anyone can do. It may be simple, but it is also powerful!

Exercise 6: "Chill Out and Get In" Meditation

1. Once again, sitting comfortably as you did in the breathing exercise, close your eyes and focus on your breathing. (Meditation will build on the breathing process, and you should do the breathing each time you go into meditation.)

2. Now take three cleansing breaths, as you did before, and focus your mind only on the breathing process, allowing your body to relax and letting all tension flow from the top of your head to the tip of your toes.

3. If any thoughts come into your mind as you continue to breathe and relax, don't try to fight them. Just allow them to happen, and when you remember you're supposed to be meditating, not thinking, go back to focusing on your breathing. Do this each time thoughts try to crowd you out of your peaceful state. Eventually, you'll be able to let the thoughts go easily, and in time, they won't be a problem at all. Practice makes perfect!

4. Once you're in meditation, allow your body and mind to come out of it on its own. At first, you'll only sustain meditation for a few minutes, maybe five. That's enough. If you wish, you can develop your meditation skills and extend the time to a half-hour. The benefits are great. But for our purposes, five to fifteen minutes are more than enough.

The next two psychic power tools build on the meditation process. In fact, once you're in meditation, the manifesting begins.

Psychic Power Tool 3: Visualization

It's really true that what we can see, we can have. The power to see pictures in our mind is one of our greatest psychic abilities. We can all see these pictures. You see them vividly in your dreams every night. We're about to do some daydreaming, of a sort, to help us get the things we desire.

The idea here is to form or create a picture in your mind of what you want. This sends a message to your subconscious mind and begins to reprogram it. The images reinforce your thoughts and add fuel to them. They work nonverbally, so you don't even need to say a thing. Just allow pictures to appear in your mind and you will have this tool mastered.

To get you started, here is an exercise to help you get comfortable with the process.

Exercise 7: Now You See It . . .

Once again, this tool works through meditation. When you're in the meditative state, which means you've done tools 1 and 2 already, you add this one to send your true request out into the Universe through your subconscious. To develop this tool, we are going to allow our subconscious mind to send our conscious mind any pictures it wishes. Do this exercise every day if you do not have success the first time. For some people it takes longer, but it will work and soon you will be treated to some spectacular sights.

1. Close your eyes, do your proper breathing, and then move into your meditation.

2. When you feel you are in a higher state of relaxation and calmness, eliminate all thoughts and drift into silent meditation.

3. Now relax and allow pictures to begin to form in your mind. In your mind's eye, see the scene I am about to describe developing until it becomes a vivid image. As you relax, feel a wave of peaceful energy moving from the top of your head to the tip of your toes. Feel your body totally relaxing. Now become aware of a cloud of white light gently swirling around you. Feel it. See it as it swirls like a billowing cloud around your body. Now, as the cloud begins to swirl and fade away, you find yourself in a beautiful, special place out in nature. You may be at the ocean, on the banks of a gently flowing river, in a garden, a meadow, or in a forest. Go wherever you wish, this is your space. Look around as it forms before your eyes. The colors of the water, the sky, and the earth are now coming into view and they are more lovely and vivid than you have ever seen. Smell the air. Feel the soft breezes caressing your body. Sit down in this special place and enjoy the sights for a moment. Drink in the beauty of nature and take note of how wonderful it all is. Relax and allow your mind and body to be at peace.

Now, take a deep breath and see the gentle white cloud swirling up from your feet making its way slowly to the top of your head. As it moves up, your sacred meditation place begins to fade from your sight. When the white cloud reaches your head, the picture disappears, the cloud fades from sight, and you return to full consciousness, relaxed and refreshed.

If you have trouble visualizing, keep trying. You need to build your visualization and meditation muscles just as you would your physical ones, so don't give up. This process becomes a natural part of you and eventually spontaneous pictures form without any help from your conscious mind.

Later in the book, you will learn to create specific visualizations, spiritual pictures, that will help you draw your desires into your life. It's as easy as daydreaming, but much more productive!

Now you're ready to add another element to your meditation and visualization—your intuitive perception.

Psychic Power Tool 4: Intuition

We're all familiar with our intuition. We've had it since we were born. It's that little nagging voice we hear in our head that tells us we should or shouldn't do something—that voice that comes from the pit of your stomach and bugs you now and again. Usually, when your intuition strikes, you're faced with a decision. Should you spend that $200 on tickets to a Broadway show when you really need new tires for your car? Or should you take piano lessons because it's more practical than what you really want, which is to study the tuba?

Our intuitive self acts within us every day. How often do we listen to it? That's the key to your success. If you listen, you'll be guided correctly. It's just so hard for most of us to trust it, because it seems to defy logic. We are logical animals, particularly in this American culture. Oriental and Eastern cultures lend themselves more readily to living this way, but we have to learn to trust our inner voice. It's correct because it knows a lot more than our conscious minds do. It's in direct communication with the Higher Power. You could say that it is the part of you that is brilliant and perfect and in the image of God. It's the spiritual you, trying to get past the intellectual you. It is wiser, and much more accurate.

In getting what you want, you need to learn to pay attention to your intuition. Then you can help to make things happen consciously. This is tough, because you'll want to ignore your intuition, to tell it to go away and leave you alone. But don't. Instead, listen to it, take its advice. You'll be glad you did.

So go ahead and buy the Broadway tickets. You might find that the money you need for the tires comes easily from another source, or your mother gives you tires for your birthday! If you listen to your intuition, your life begins to balance and you won't get hurt. You will only get hurt when you ignore it, buy the tires, and feel deprived because you really want a night out at the theater. And go ahead and study the tuba. You may become a virtuoso at it, land a concert contract, and your life could be changed forever. If not, you may have given up the piano and music altogether because you were unhappy.

I can honestly say that my intuition has never steered me wrong. When I realized how much it could help me get what I wanted, I learned to trust and use it and I always get excellent results.

What follows are ways in which you can add power to your manifesting by simply observing, listening to your inner voice, and recognizing what is going on around you. In doing so, you demonstrate that you are focused, ready, and willing to receive all that you request.

Exercise 8: That Little Birdie in Your Ear

1. After you've done your breathing, meditation, and visualization, and you are out of meditation into consciousness, tell yourself that you will begin to *recognize* the prompting of your intuition and you will *trust* that it will help you get what you want.

2. Next, look for the signs that things are beginning to happen in your everyday life to make your wish come true. For instance, after asking for my Jeep, I inadvertently drove by a dealership and out of the blue my dad, who was in the car with me, said, "Just for fun, let's go test-drive one of those." We did, and one hour later, I was a proud owner.

3. Don't go against your gut feelings, ever. Don't ignore them. *Pay attention.* Do this every minute of every day until you get what you want.

We Ain't Done Yet

So there you have it: the basics of getting everything you ever wanted. They defy logic. They are purely spiritual and they work. You now have enough information to get started. But if you want to get really good at it and eliminate all chance of failure, you'll need to keep reading. In the following chapters, I'll give you skills to add to these basic tools, tell you how to incorporate those skills into your manifesting and your life, and help you to identify any spiritual roadblocks you may have that could stand in your way. If you are committed and willing to learn to use your psychic common sense, getting everything you ever wanted is just a matter of time.

CHAPTER 4

Tapping Into Your Power

*G*etting your heart's desire requires you to send your message out to the Universe on more than one channel. That means you've got to pack a lot of power in your punch! First, you've got to find that power, then direct and focus it on your intention or the essence of what you want to materialize. The best and most effective way to do that is to use words and pictures.

In order to accomplish our goals we need the help of the tremendous power that lies within us. It's sometimes called our will, inner strength, higher self, or even God. It will support us once we recognize and acknowledge it and demonstrate that we're up to the task ahead. It's really quite simple. We've got to believe and trust in our own ability to receive the things we want in this lifetime.

I can almost hear that voice inside you saying, "Yeah, yeah, yeah, but will it really work?" I'm here to tell you it does. Trust is the most important element in this whole process. Eliminate the negative thoughts that say, "It can't be done." Each time you give in to a negative thought, you zap your power. Each time you buy into someone else's negativity, you take a step backward in your spiritual growth. For instance, when you allow another person to stop you from pursuing your dreams of a career, or the relocation of your home, or a long-desired adventure you'd like to try, you allow their fears, their reservations, or sometimes their jealousy to become more important than your needs.

When you trust that you have what it takes to get what you want, and that there is some kind of spiritual order to the Universe, then you can truly begin to draw on your own personal power. If you believe that everything happens in life for a reason, it gets easier to accept your abilities. If you do your prep work and eliminate people or situations from your life that are negative and drain you of your enthusiasm, you will get rid of the doubt and truly see that all things are possible.

Having said all that, you'll need to zero in on what you *truly* want. To become real, our desires must form deep within the core of our being. We must acknowledge what lies beneath the surface, in the heart of our request.

Understand the Essence of Your Intention

Whatever you want, it will only come to you if you truly want it with every fiber of your being. It is not enough to give lip service to an idea. You've really got to want it in your heart and soul. Lots of times we feel we want something and later on, after thinking about it, we realize we didn't want it at all. I'm convinced that that's where the line, "Be careful what you wish for, you just might get it," came from. It is all about *knowing*—knowing, without a doubt, the very essence of what you want. It is only then that you can get it.

The essence or basis of what you want is what I'm talking about. For instance, if you think you want lots of money in your life, think again. Are your bills always greater than your income? Can you never make ends meet? Do you have a good job but there's never enough money in your bank account to cover all your expenses with some left for fun? These troubles could describe a person who is fortunate in that he or she has a good job but is creating struggle and scarcity in life. It is not really a lot of money this person needs, but financial security. For instance, let's assume you feel that if you had a certain sum of money your struggles would be over and your finances would stabilize. Let's say that amount was $10,000. You then ask for and receive it from the Universe, but when that's gone you are right back where you started. Rather, it is better to ask for an end to struggle and scarcity—then you won't need the $10,000 at all because you will have removed the problem. The essence of this intention is financial security, prosperity, and abundance. Ask for something greater than just a sum of money and you'll be creating lifelong happiness. Try creating all the wealth you'll ever need, instead of getting a limited amount. That way you will always have enough for everything you want. Think about that.

Here's another example of finding the essence of your intention. If you are ill with a particular disease or ailment, instead of asking for it to be cured, ask for the essence of it, which would be perfect health. If you create perfect health, you will never need to create a particular cure.

One of my dearest clients and a member of my small but mighty metaphysical church fell quite ill. He had been in fine shape for the year I had known him, then one day, I received a call telling me he had been hospitalized for internal bleeding. The doctors couldn't stop the bleeding, and couldn't find the cause. He was near death, receiving blood transfusions daily for a week. During service that Sunday, he lay in his hospital bed and we, his friends, with Spirit, sent him positive healing energy, our form of healing prayer. We didn't pray to stop the bleeding, but we prayed for the essence of what we wished for him, which was that he return to perfect health.

The Tuesday following, our friend called me and told me a remarkable story. At 11:20 A.M. that past Sunday, which was the precise time we had all begun sending our healing energy to him, the curtains in his intensive care room began to move. There was no one there. As the curtain slowly began to open, a burst of energy, as he called it, entered the room and he could feel himself responding to the thoughts we sent him. He felt better, and by the next day the bleeding stopped. By the weekend, he was home and in full recovery. Two weeks later, he was back to work, with no sign of the problem left in his body.

This man's doctors cannot understand how and why he has been restored to health, but to this day, two years later, he remains healthy. He has since told me that he believes he'll never have a serious physical problem again because he intends to have perfect health for the rest of this lifetime.

I know you're thinking that this is an unusual case, but I am here to tell you it is not. Anyone can create health, financial security, or love. You've simply got to realize what is at the heart of what you want. That is your true intention, your true essence. Don't limit yourself. Create what will be in your highest and greatest good, and the good of all the other people concerned in the situation. Be clear. The Universe supports whatever you create or ask for, because It/God wants you to have bliss and be happy. That's the true order of things.

Where Do We Begin?

All creation begins in the mind. Thought produces physical reality. Courage and tenacity get results. Pictures begin in the mind. Form pictures of yourself in your mind as though you have already achieved what you desire. See yourself successful, thin, rich, or happy. Your original idea is the nucleus for growth and manifestation in your life. When it is completed, thought becomes more than what it was. It becomes reality.

Knowing what you want, identifying the essence of your intention, will create successful results. Confusion creates mediocre or nonexistent results. That is why you sometimes get what you want, and sometimes you don't. You might not have understood your intention. Spend time thinking about what you want. It must be definite and heartfelt.

Here's an exercise to help you to form your intentions and find the essence of your desires. You can do this in your working journal, as well.

Exercise 9: What's My Essence?

Record your decisions about the following statements:

1. Decide on one aspect of your present reality you would like to change.

    _____

    _____

    _____

    _____

    _____

    _____

    _____

    _____

    _____

2. Put it into a sentence that has special meaning to you alone.
    Examples: "I want to get rid of my asthma."
    "I want $1,500 to pay my credit card bills."
    "I want to meet the man of my dreams and get married."

    _____

    _____

    _____

    _____

    _____

    _____

    _____

    _____

3. Now, having written your desire, we'll discover your true essence or intention. Look at the list that follows. See what these wants become when they are translated into true intentions.

Want	Essence/True Intention
To get rid of asthma.	To be in perfect health.
To get $1,500 to pay bills.	To have as much money as you'll ever need.
To find a mate and get married.	To attract romantic love into your life,
	or
	To end loneliness.

Do you see how that's done? Boil it down, and face your reality. Now you try it with your own intentions before reading on. Pretty soon you'll get to the heart of everything you've ever wanted. You might be surprised that there are some things you really don't want or need at all.

Say It, See It, and Send It

You have soul-searched, contemplated, ruminated over, and discovered the deepest essence of your desires. You understand your intentions and are ready to connect directly to your own power source to begin using it to your greatest advantage. *Say It, See It,* and *Send It* is a useful method in developing your inner mastery. It's easy to remember and focuses upon the awesome strength of your mind. This method works like a cosmic magnet in drawing people, situations, and events into your life to help you get what you want. We must literally practice all three elements of the method together. They must be done as part of your manifesting ritual. In the next several chapters I'll be explaining them individually.

So what better place to start than at the beginning? *Say It* focuses on how to put our desires into words, how to write requests effectively (you didn't know there was a right way and a wrong way, did you?) and how to use the power of the written and spoken word to assist us in getting our needs met.

Say It: Giving a Voice to Your Request

In the realm of the metaphysical, we put our essence or true intention into the form of a request known as an affirmation. An affirmation is nothing more than a sentence or group of sentences notifying the Universe that we're in need and focusing our mind on our specific goal. They pack a spiritual wallop and are a form of prayer to many. But affirmations don't require you to be religious. They work in two ways: first, by the sheer act of formal declaration we announce our intention to the Universe/God/the Source, etc., and second, we reprogram our own subconscious mind in the process. In other words, *we begin to change the way we think*. Our subconscious mind is a tough cookie. The subconscious takes time to understand our message and needs repetition in order to adapt. This means that affirmations must be said and repeated often so we can transform our thoughts, which then help to redirect the course of our life. We end up creating the exact situation we are affirming.

Here's how it works. We literally tell our subconscious mind that we already have what we are asking for. In other words we *think* and *act* as though we already have the new job, new love, or money by *saying* that we do. So instead of sending a message that is requesting something, affirmations send a message that simply require support from the Universe. In this way, the Universe gives us what it understands as more of the same, even though it may be new to us. This is not as tough to follow as it appears. I'll explain.

To affirm or give spiritual mind power to our intention we focus our thoughts on the fact that what we want is already ours. Here's an example of an affirmation to lift depression that will shed some light on this new way of thinking: "I am happy and joyful and living a fulfilling life." The words are positive, simple, and strong. They convey a sense of power within the individual declaring them. This person is confident and trusting that what he or she wants is already a part of his life, waiting to show itself in material form—waiting to become reality.

When the Universe receives the message, it responds by creating and making available specific situations that will result in the sender of the affirmation actually becoming happy, joyful, and fulfilled.

This is a strange concept to many. "How does saying I already have something draw it to me?" you ask. Well, remember that the Universe will support whatever you want. If you say you already have something in your life, the Universe will give you support for it or more reasons to continue to declare it.

The simple spiritual fact is that anything we want or need is ours already because the Power or Source (God, if you will) is within us and this creative center can do it all. We just need to bring it forward so we can see it in our physical life, rather than just knowing it in our mind.

As kids, many of us were taught that a Greater Power could do anything, but we might not have understood that we are actually a part of that power and we can call upon it at anytime to show itself in our everyday lives. We may not realize that we don't have to wait for a miracle, we can create one!

You see, we think a whole lot faster than the physical world moves. We can have a thought in a split second, but it takes time for that thought to be executed in the material world. For instance, you wake up one morning and decide you'd like to go on a picnic that day. You imagine how beautiful your favorite picnic spot is, the loveliness of the weather, the fun you will have, the taste of the good food you will eat, and you have many other thoughts that in a way predict the future of your day. You can almost see your day in your mind's eye. Then you do all the necessary tasks to make it happen. You call a friend to join you, you make a delicious lunch, you pack a cooler, you load the car, and you're off. The full extent of what you've envisioned hasn't happened yet in the physical world—you're not at the picnic grounds—but you already know the outcome. You're just waiting for your physical world to catch up with your mind. That's what we're doing when we create and say an affirmation and then wait for it to manifest in our life. When you say an affirmation, it's the same as preparing for the picnic. You already know the outcome you desire, and you're waiting for it to show up in your life so you talk and act as if there's no doubt that it'll happen.

Creating and saying affirmations takes faith. It takes trust in the order of the Universe. We have to believe that what we need is already ours and is simply in the works developing, growing, and than finally materializing. That's the basis of manifesting. It's not all that complicated but it does take commitment and the skill to write affirmations that get results. The only way to get what you want is through clear, focused thinking. Scattered thoughts get us nowhere because an unclear statement produces an unclear or ineffective end. If we have a specific goal, we need a specific affirmation, one that's free of doubt and ambiguity. Once you get the hang of writing affirmations, the easier it gets and the faster they'll work. By the end of this chapter you'll be a pro. It's all in the wording.

I use affirmations in my own personal manifesting and in my spiritual counseling practice. They're part of my daily routine and I start out each day with one or two. Affirmations are not only used in manifesting but they are also helpful in maintaining a happy, positive life. They can be written as a simple expression of motivation in our lives to help keep us going, as a source of clarity and consolation in tough times, and to thank the Universe for moving and working in our lives, just as prayers do.

My clients and church members are always sharing the happy results of using affirmations. Each week I hold an evening lecture and meditation class. At the end of it I hand out an affirmation based upon my topic for the evening. Everyone enjoys them and they tell me they even look forward to saying them because it is a tangible way to feel in control of their lives and futures. This is much stronger than some types of prayer that beseech or beg for a response. Affirmations don't wait—they create.

One of my students recently wanted to change careers and find a position more suited to her new sense of spirituality. She created an affirmation during a class exercise, combined it with the other steps included in this book, and saw quick results. Two months later she was preparing to relocate to her new and exciting job, a career much better suited to her new way of thinking.

Another client was fighting cancer. I use affirmations as a mainstay in my spiritual energy healings. When we began working together, the cancer was spreading rapidly. We used affirmations that affirmed her return to perfect health. She repeated these daily and within six months the cancer had gone into remission. She is now virtually cancer-free.

I can't restate enough how important affirmations are. When you begin using them, you'll know for yourself.

Creating the Message

Once you understand the essence of your desire, you can get specific. Affirming what you want by stating it plainly and clearly sends a strong message to your subconscious, but it also works on your conscious mind as well. When we hear with our inner ear, our "mind's ear," we tend to register what we've heard. Our words become our reality. In order to get what we want we have to mean what we say. So, in putting together an affirmation, we've got to be perfectly sure of what we want.

An affirmation is nothing more than a few sentences that restate our desire. Doing this right requires a positive attitude and a belief that what you are asking for can be yours.

This is a sample affirmation for getting a new car. In fact, it's the one I used to manifest my new car back in 1993. It is very specific. The essence of my desire was for trouble-free, affordable, personal transportation. By the way, it worked within two days.

> *I am the owner of a new 1993 black Jeep Cherokee. I am able to afford it, I have the down payment, I get credit easily, and payments are low and easy for me to meet. I thank the Universe for this Jeep, which is already mine and has come to me in a safe and loving way. I receive this or something better, in my highest and greatest good, and that of all concerned, in accordance with divine will and the free will of all concerned. And so it is!*

Let's take a look at the components of this affirmation.

Request

> *I am the owner of a new 1993 black Jeep Cherokee. I am able to afford it, I have the down payment, I get credit easily, and payments are low and easy for me to meet.*

Of course you would put in your own request, in detail, but the positive language is what's important here. Make your desire known to the Universe in a simple, detailed sentence. Include the essence of what you want, and any

74

specifics. In this case, I wanted a Jeep, but I had some very important conditions that had to be met in order to make owning it comfortable for me. Don't overlook the implications of your request. I needed a car that I could afford, the down payment, easy credit, and low monthly payments. I didn't want to struggle just to keep it. Make sure you think ahead when you form your request.

Express gratitude

I thank the Universe (God/Goddess/the Source, etc.)
for this Jeep, which is already mine . . .

Affirmations need another very important intention included within them: gratitude. We need to express our appreciation to the Universe, God, etc., for listening to our request and enabling it to become a part of our lives. It's not good policy to take Spirit for granted. I always include a phrase of thanks. You can add your thanks anywhere within the affirmation.

We must always thank the power in the Universe, whatever you call it, that works with us. Being grateful sends the message to this Greater Power that we are grateful now, and that we know our prayer is answered the minute we have the desire. That is indicated by the words, "already mine." We are stating, in no uncertain terms, that we are confident we will receive what we want, it is already in the works for us, and that it will be part of our physical world shortly. It gives the Universe a strong reason to boost our already strong nature. We don't plead, we expect. We know that the Divine wants us to have a happy life and is thrilled to enable us to achieve it.

Gratitude does more than simply thank, it draws things to us. It is attractive. You may have heard people observe that when things are going well in their lives they just keep getting better. They're on a roll, as they say. Gratitude to Spirit starts you rolling and, sooner or later, you are given more and more reasons to be grateful. But, of course, your gratitude must be heartfelt, not faked. Just saying the words is not enough, you must really mean them.

Protect

... and has come to me in a safe and loving way ...

Protection is a scary word. In this case, it is nothing to be upset about. By protection I mean that you are asking for your request to be answered without negative consequences. For instance, some years ago an associate of mine asked to receive a new radio for her car with a cassette player (this was long before the days of CD players). She asked that it come to her free of charge, but she neglected to ask that it come to her in a safe and loving way. The result was not what she expected. Someone smashed her car window and stole her old radio right out of the dashboard. Her new radio was free because the insurance company paid to replace the stolen one. She shuddered at the thought that her mind was so powerful.

I, myself, have neglected to include this very important phrase and suffered for it. About two years ago, I decided to ask the Universe for a vacation. I was on overload, working too hard at three jobs, and I was exhausted. I asked that I be given time off, without having to go to work, anywhere. Just a couple of weeks would be fine, I mused. I left out that I wanted this time to come to me in a safe and loving way. I got two weeks off, all right—bedridden, with the worst flu I'd ever had. I couldn't enjoy myself or go anywhere! I learned that it is far better to include this step than take a chance.

Remove limits

... I receive this or something better, in my highest and greatest good, and that of all concerned ...

It is important to open up to more than we've asked for, to ask for "this or something better." That way, you're telling the Universe that if a 1993 Jeep Cherokee is unavailable, you'll take a 1993 Jeep Grand Cherokee instead.

That'll be okay with you. In other words, you'll accept another vehicle that may be more expensive or has more options, etc. See? Never limit your request. Allow for something better. This gives the Universe a chance to get you something you want sooner, if what you've requested isn't immediately available. I don't know about you, but I'm happy with getting more, faster.

Adding "in my highest and greatest good, and that of all concerned" further removes limitations by letting the Universe guide you in a positive way to your highest potential. If the Jeep is not the best car for you, then the Universe will supply the one that is. It will be just fine with you, because you are willing to accept the essence of what you want, if the specifics aren't available.

Acknowledge

. . . in accordance with divine will and the free will
of all concerned . . .

Here you recognize that there is a Greater Power at work in your life and a greater plan in process, and you acknowledge that what comes to you is in line with that plan or divine will. You also affirm that your request is made of your own free will. The free will of others is included here in that it will take other people and their intervention to get your request to you and you need their cooperation. In order to get my Jeep, I needed the free will decision of the salesman, the dealership manager, and the loan company—plenty of free will decisions that could have swung against me, don't you think? Imagine the number of free wills I had to consider in the publishing and selling of this book, and all of the folks involved in making it happen. The thought is astounding. I even had to consider your free will as a consumer. When you acknowledge the help and free will of others, you cover all your possibilities and remove any attempts at manipulation, which allows all of it to flow to you easily.

Finalize

. . . And so it is!

You say once again that you believe you already have what you desire, and that in your consciousness it is done, with the words, "And so it is." This is a metaphysical way of saying "Amen" or "So be it." You can use those if you like. Whatever is comfortable. It caps the whole thing off nicely, don't you think?

You don't have to write your affirmations exactly as this one, as long as you include the basics I have outlined:

- Request

- Express Gratitude

- Protect

- Remove limits

- Acknowledge

- Finalize

Before you set your spiritual requests in motion, we'll look at some other examples of affirmations and fine-tune the wording of our requests. You need to express your desires in your own voice. These are just suggestions. Choose the words that ring true and are comfortable for you.

Power Talk

The affirmation is always written using positive language that motivates and declares our intention to the powers that be. You could say it's a spiritual broadcast that carries our intention across the waves of time and space. If you use negative words, you get negative results. Writing affirmations is easy once you get used to the system.

It's important to use simple, clear language that gets to the point in a hurry. Don't be flowery or cute. We don't want to confuse the issue. Tell the Universe straight out what you want.

Another common downfall of many of my students and clients is that they try to combine more than one intention into one affirmation. This scatters the energy and it loses power. *Use only one request per affirmation.* Of course, when you get good at manifesting you can have more than one request in the works at the same time, but it's not a good idea for beginners. Start slowly, there's plenty of time.

Getting Down to Business

Let's say you want to get a new job or career. You can write your affirmation in several forms, being specific or general in your intention. Here are a couple of ways to begin using the six basic elements outlined above. You'll notice that those basics can be combined in any one sentence in the following affirmations:

I thank the Universe (God/Goddess/my higher self/the Source/All There Is) for my perfect career. I attract the perfect career for me. My perfect career using my very special talents is already mine, and comes to me in a safe and loving way according to divine will and the free will of all concerned. This is so. And so it is.

or,

A new job that is right and perfect for me is already mine. I know that the Universe (God/my higher self/the Source, you choose) is already sending my new job to me. I am at peace knowing it is so, in a safe and loving way, in accordance with divine will and the

free will of all concerned. I thank the Universe
(God/Goddess, etc.) for this gift. So be it.

Taking the first affirmation apart, you can see how the basics can be combined into one sentence, if you like.

- "I thank the Universe (God/Goddess/my higher self/the Source/All There Is) for my perfect career." (request, gratitude)

- "I attract the perfect career for me." (Removes limitations by leaving you open to any number of wonderful possibilities, or you can ask for a specific career and add, "or something better.")

- "My perfect career using my very special talents is already mine, and comes to me in a safe and loving way according to divine will and the free will of all concerned." (protection, gratitude, acknowledgment)

- "This is so. And so it is." (final affirmation)

You see that the affirmation covers all of the necessary points. As I have said, you don't absolutely need to use these exact words as long as you capture the essence of those crucial elements. We'll analyze the second version next.

- "A new job that is right and perfect for me is already mine. I know that the Universe (God/my higher self/the Source, you choose) is already sending my new job to me." (request, gratitude, removal of limits)

- "I am at peace knowing it is so, in a safe and loving way . . ." (protect)

- ". . . in accordance with divine will and the free will of all concerned." (acknowledge)

- "I thank the Universe (God/Goddess, etc.) for this gift." (gratitude)

- "So be it." (final affirmation)

You will not need to dissect your affirmations to this degree once you get used to writing them, but it does help to follow this plan when you're in training. And speaking of training, it's about time that you tried your hand at your own affirmations. Look back at your notes from the earlier chapters and choose one priority in your life you would like to manifest, or think of a new one. Use it to write your first affirmation and you'll be on the road to creating your ideal life before you know it.

Exercise 10: Speak Your Truth— Writing Your Affirmations

What's your intention? What do you want to draw into your life? State it here in a few words, or use your journal.

_____

_____

_____

_____

_____

_____

_____

_____

_____

_____

Using some of the words you wrote above, begin to construct a positive statement that embodies your true desire. Get to the heart of it and use simple, clear language (this is not the affirmation, but just a simple sentence that you feel expresses what you want).

_____

_____

_____

_____

_____

_____

_____

_____

_____

Rewrite the above ideas using the crucial elements: request, express gratitude, protect, remove limits, acknowledge, finalize. You can always go back and reword these, just give each point a try.

Request

_____

_____

_____

_____

_____

_____

_____

_____

_____

Express Gratitude

_____

_____

_____

_____

_____

_____

_____

_____

_____

Protect

_____

_____

_____

_____

_____

_____

_____

_____

_____

Remove Limits

_____
_____
_____
_____
_____
_____
_____
_____
_____
_____

Acknowledge

_____
_____
_____
_____
_____
_____
_____
_____
_____
_____
_____

Finalize

Now write your completed affirmation by combining all the significant parts into a cohesive paragraph, just as in the examples.

There you have it, your first desire put into words and ready for action. This is the most time-consuming and difficult part of the manifestation process. From here on, it's quite easy.

You'll have to practice until you get used to writing this way. Once you do it'll become second nature, and you will have mastered a skill that's rewarding spiritually, mentally, and physically. When you're in command of this technique you can help loved ones and friends develop their own affirmations. It's a gift you can share with everyone and I encourage you to do so.

Eventually we'll use our affirmations in our manifesting ritual. They will literally be spoken by you out loud, as well as repeated in your head. Speaking them aloud sends an even stronger message to the Universe. It breaks through our Earth's dense physical atmosphere like radio waves, and your desire takes flight on a vibration that is faster and can make its way to higher planes of existence, such as the astral plane, where thought resides. It's here where our intention takes shape. When it reaches this level, our request has formally been registered with the Universe. Then it's just a matter of time before that intention becomes a physical reality.

You'll soon see how affirmations fit into a six-step process to getting everything you ever wanted in chapter 10. In chapter 13 I've included a comprehensive list of tried and tested sure-fire affirmations that get results. Resist the urge to jump ahead. Affirmations can be more effective when you write them yourself. It's an energy thing, you know.

When written well, affirmations get amazing results and nothing can stop them. They're very powerful. Soon you'll see for yourself.

Now What?

Now that you have such great command of the written word and know that once verbalized and voiced your intention cannot be stopped, we're even going to tap into more power within you.

Fasten your seat belts; we're about to take off on a journey within your mind. In our mind's eye we can create pictures of what we want that are so vivid they can't help but become real. Our next chapter focuses on *See It*, the second very powerful part of our method.

CHAPTER 5

Giving What You Want a Face

$\mathcal{N}$ow that we have realized and harnessed the might of the written and spoken word, it is time to unleash the energy of the mind. *Thoughts are things.* They have the power to create tangible, physical changes, and can impact the course of our lives tremendously. Thoughts themselves are things in the sense that they are statements of the mind that precede their actualization in the physical, material world. They are the seeds, when planted, that blossom into expression in our daily world as events, circumstances, and matter. The chair you are sitting in while reading this book was a thought in the mind of someone in the past who was tired of sitting on the ground! The idea might have been generated by the need for comfort or convenience (tree stumps are hard to come by in a pinch). Whatever the case, this ancient person had a single vision that changed the course of history. We might not make such a profound contribution to humankind in our own personal manifesting efforts, but nevertheless our thoughts can change our destiny.

When we think a thought, our mind does something automatically with that information. It forms a picture. Just for a moment, think of the pictures your mind forms when someone describes a hot fudge sundae to you. Heaps of creamy chocolate ice cream (my personal favorite) topped with a generous helping of dreamy, delicious, hot, thick fudge. Not to mention the final glorious, fluffy, white, satin, whipped cream (nuts and cherry are optional). It sounds so good you can almost taste it. Please, don't drop the book and run to your local Dairy Queen, we have work to do. This vision is a motivator. It piques your interest, stimulates your basic, physical desires, and urges you to take action.

Mental images have been used in our society for ages. For example, a political campaign counts on your ability to visualize the beautiful, affluent, abundant, peaceful life of the future its candidate promises so that you'll get out and vote. Open any newspaper or magazine and you are bombarded with images of all kinds trying to get you to spend your hard-earned dollars simply by suggesting that the girl or guy with the straight, white teeth in the toothpaste ad, enjoying the high life, could actually be you for $1.89.

Besides words, pictures *outside* of your mind help you to form pictures *inside* your mind. We can look at pictures that depict desires similar to ours and allow that image to influence our manifesting through a sort of visual-mind osmosis. I'll get into more of that later, with specific techniques.

For now, it is important to learn that visual images, stimulated externally or created within your own mind, can work for you, putting the power of your future back into your own hands. We can improve our lives by learning how to describe, in detail, what we want in words, and then allowing the picture to form in our minds.

Creating the image of our desired outcome, or visualizing, is the next very powerful step in getting what you want in life. In this chapter, we will discover how to influence the flow of energy in the Universe by envisioning and owning it. This second step, *See It,* describes the specific methods of visualization and meditation used to draw your desires into your life. If you can think it, you can have it!

See It

Let's begin our journey into consciousness by learning some very basic skills. *You have to literally tell your mind what you want to see.* So many of my students insist that they cannot visualize. To this, I say, "Bunk!" If you have trouble creating mental pictures, it is probably because:

- you're trying too hard,

- expecting it to be more difficult than it is, or

- blocking the images for a hidden, psychological reason, like you don't feel you really deserve to have it all.

Granted, many of us are visual people, meaning we learn better predominantly through impulses that affect our eyes. Research has been done that confirms it is easier for these people to visualize in the mind's eye then those who are primarily audio (hearing) learners or kinesthetic (physical, hands-on) learners. But research also states that each person exhibits characteristics of all three of these learning types, so there are no excuses.

You may not be a person who is excuse-prone, but you just might have a legitimate mental barrier to getting all you want in life. There is hope for you. It's time we talked about removing those barriers and clearing your path to bliss. Unless you work on removing your blocks to manifesting, you will not be successful at it. Visualization, the heart of this chapter, can be cut short or rendered ineffective if you harbor doubt or fear of any kind. Writing affirmations, as you did in the previous chapter, is a logical process, but meditation and imaging are intuitive/psychic processes that require faith, trust, and practice. Most people are just not used to using their intuition in place of logic. When you master this ability, you are actually using more of your brain power—the invisible, spiritual part of you. That part is directly connected to the Universe —a hotline to God!

Visualization demands that we follow the prompting of our inner voice and let it flow freely. If a person is afraid to let go of their conscious control, they will limit their abundance, joy, wealth, good health, love, and all the wonderful gifts of the Universe by creating subconscious impediments to their success in all areas of life. Removing blocks removes limitations because it allows us to create our abundance from deeper, more powerful, concentrated forces that exist within our psyche.

Your physical world and logical mind are only parts of your entire existence. We know that we only use about ten percent of our brain power. This manifesting process expands your brain power and uses more of it, hence making your thoughts more powerful. You will need to get over any doubts in your mind that thoughts, your mental energy, can most definitely affect your physical world. Removing questions and strengthening your resolve will enable you to meditate, visualize, and create miracles without hesitation.

Unlock the Block

It is true that you can sabotage your own success because of an inner obstacle. These blocks appear as doubts and fears. You can unlock your block with positive thinking. Believing you can have it all and taking the necessary action to make it happen is your key. It is necessary to quiet your conscious mind and allow God, often known as your higher self, spiritual mind, or divine mind, to take over. No action is more powerful than that! Doubt and fear can easily be overcome by your faith in the tremendous strength within you. You can do your part in removing these debilitating emotions by voicing affirmative statements to clear them.

Even if you are not blocked, it helps to reaffirm your openness by using an affirmation before you go into a manifesting visualization meditation. Say the following affirmation for opening and clearing your psychic channel.

Doubt and fear are no longer a part of my consciousness.
The Universe (God/Goddess/the Source, etc.) removes them now.
Whatever I want comes to me through the divine power within
me. I am open and willing to receive my highest and greatest
good. And so it is (so be it, amen, so mote it be, etc.).

Say this psychic commonsense affirmation with all your heart, every day, as many times as it takes until you really believe it. Yell it out if you have to, and convince your stubborn conscious mind that it is true. One of the best places to practice this affirmation is in your car, provided the windows are closed. I find that my car provides a safe environment for vigorous expression, if you know what I mean. Anyway, just say it with such gusto that your emotions, as well as the words, remove the blocks. It works. Try it now, before you read on.

(I mean it. Do it now. We will take this time out for a hearty affirmation break!)

Now, how are you? Feels good, doesn't it? It's that simple. Reprogram your doubts and fears, tell them they no longer have control over you, and press on. Keep going. Your spirit is more powerful than those nasty doubts. Even if they persist, get louder in your affirming and eliminate them from your mind. Be patient. Sooner or later, through your sheer persistence, they will recur less frequently until you are able to eliminate them by simply and gently willing them away. Your stubborn subconscious mind, which feeds these blocks to your conscious mind, has no choice but to succumb. You've outyelled and outsmarted it.

Back to Business

Now that you have eliminated the mental obstacles, your mind is free to create. If you still have problems visualizing, it just might be that you're trying too hard. It would be best to take a break from your meditation and try again later.

When all else fails, there is still a way. You can help your mind visualize easily by saying the words to yourself that describe what you want to be seeing. Then, it is a matter of relaxing and letting your mind flow.

In doing this work, I have found that images need *you* to get them going. A common cry of students is, "But it feels like I'm making it up." Guess what? You are! You are the author of this play. Visualization works best in a calm environment and meditation. In this relaxed state, you *must* form the necessary images in order to control the outcome. If you were to allow your imagination to take the lead, you could get off track and lose sight of your true intention, the one you worked so hard on forming in chapter 4.

Mental imaging is not an exercise in creative writing. You need to control it in order to be focused. Scattered pictures cause scattered results. Clarity, purpose, and direction are all important in manifesting your needs and wants.

For a moment, imagine that your true intention is to draw the perfect job for you. Let's say your interests and talents are in public service, particularly social work. Public service is a very broad spectrum. If you don't control your images, you could go into meditation with a nice, conservative, future picture in mind, such as seeing yourself working with underprivileged youth, in a job you love, or cashing a very fat paycheck, but your mind begins to wander. You suddenly see yourself before a great crowd of people, about to give a moving, earth-shattering speech demanding justice for the downtrodden. After your talk, you are whisked away into a limousine that takes you home to the White House. A bit dramatic, but you see how a good intention can turn into a fantasy of disjointed dreams (unless, of course, your intention is to actually *be* the president of the United States, in which case this visualization will work beautifully)!

Practically speaking, keep your emotions and imaging under control by carefully detailing the events in your mind. It helps to write down your detailed image, particularly if you are one of those people who has trouble relaxing. Nerves can cause us to be too impatient to simply wait for the pictures to form. You must try very hard to calm down, relax, and trust yourself. Don't let your nerves create fuzzy pictures full of uncertainty. Settle down and know that what you want is truly accessible.

The following is an exercise to help you begin visualizing. The visions you create will act like magnets in the Universe, so be specific and careful. This is not a casual process. It is deliberate and calculated. You can't get what you want if you are not focused.

Exercise 11: Now You See It . . .

Meditation is the environment where visualization takes place. You are used to meditating by now, having practiced in previous chapters. We'll build on it by going through a mock visualization—in this case, an intention to manifest a new car. This is just a way for you to get used to the imaging method. When you are really manifesting your true intention, the entire scenario will be different. It will reflect your own desire, your own images and needs. So, for now, we will use the sample visualization. Also, it would really help to tape record this exercise and play it repeatedly until you are comfortable with all the necessary elements mentioned. You won't want to read it or have to open your eyes when you do this for real, or you might get distracted. Distractions could scatter your energy. In that situation, you need to go back to square one and begin again. So here goes. Who knows? You might just get yourself a new car—I did!

1. Close your eyes, relax, and find a comfortable position in your chair.

2. Take three deep breaths, inhaling through the nose and exhaling through the mouth.

3. When you feel your body relaxing, breath normally and drift into a higher state of calmness, eliminating all thoughts.

4. Now begin to form a picture in your mind. In your mind's eye, see your new car as though it were standing before you. Give it the exact color, model, year, and make that you want. View it as though it were on a movie screen. Now, expand your vision and see your shiny new car sitting in your driveway. See yourself coming out of your home, getting into your new car, and driving around. Allow your picture to gain strength by letting yourself feel the emotions of the moment. How do you feel driving your new car? Are you happy, proud, excited, relieved? Experience all of those emotions as this movie unfolds before you in your mind. The more involved you get with your picture, the stronger the signal to your subconscious. Enjoy this. Add other people to it. Hear their comments and compliments. Create a positive, beautiful, pleasing scenario. Make pretty pictures. Know that what you see now is what you will get!

5. When you are satisfied with your picture and you feel it is complete, see yourself driving into the sunset. Give your movie a happy ending. Whatever you visualize, end it happily and see yourself fulfilled.

6. As you allow the picture to fade from your mind, slowly bring yourself back to a calm, quiet state of meditation, eliminating all thought and just relaxing.

7. Now, with your mind a blank, take another deep, cleansing breath and, as you exhale, return to full consciousness and open your eyes.

If this exercise was easy for you and you had no trouble visualizing, then you can move forward without further practice. To put more power into our manifesting, we will now add the affirmations we have created previously to our meditation. Incorporating the exact words reinforces the power of the pictures we have just made and sends a strong message out to the Universe.

When we back up our pictures with words, we infuse even greater substance and might into our desires.

This next activity picks up where the former ended. You need to paint your own picture of your specific desire in your own words. When you've designed your dream, a third exercise will join them together, and you will be ready to begin your serious work. Your thoughts are now beginning to create your reality.

Exercise 12: Paint Your Picture in Words

In the following space, or in your journal, write down, in very specific detail, your own vision of what you want. Just as we did in the new car meditation, craft your own scenario. Don't leave anything out. See yourself getting what you want, enjoying it, and feeling fulfilled and satisfied. Follow the elements included in the meditation, substituting your own words.

Now that you have written your own visualization, you can take it to the next application, as we combine what we've done so far. This next exercise joins the picture to the words. It starts with the manifesting meditation, allows you to substitute your request, and then adds your personal affirmation written in chapter 4 to your meditation and visualization process.

Exercise 13: The Word's the Thing

Let's assume you have done the original new car visualization meditation described earlier. Now do it again, using your own intention/desire that you have just written, but instead of coming back to full consciousness, as in step 7, we will eliminate that step, remain in the meditative state, and add our affirmation.

Read this exercise over before you repeat your meditation using your own intention. Review the affirmation you wrote in the previous chapter and the one in this exercise, committing both to memory. That way, you will be less likely to forget what needs to be added, eliminating the need to come out of your trance state.

Note: Assume that this addition begins after step 6 in the sample meditation, in which you have already substituted the visualization you created for your own intention.

1. Now that you have completed your visualization, recall the words of your affirmation while remaining in meditation. Say them in your mind. Add emotion to the words, really feel them. Then repeat them twice more or until you are convinced beyond a doubt that they are true.

2. Allow yourself to drift back to consciousness by saying to yourself, "I am coming back to consciousness, and I thank the Universe (God/Goddess/Source, etc.) for this ability to receive what is already mine. I am conscious, relaxed, satisfied, and refreshed."

3. Finally, when you are out of meditation, immediately say your affirmation out loud three times, or until you are convinced beyond a doubt that it is true.

You have just learned the basic process of the manifesting method. If pictures are still difficult for you, what follows is a useful alternative to creating them yourself.

Outside Influences

Earlier in this chapter, I mentioned that besides words, pictures outside of your mind can help you to form pictures inside your mind. We can look at pictures that depict similar desires and allow the image to influence our manifesting through what I call visual-mind osmosis. This easy practice involves taking images that already exist and using them to give a positive suggestion to your subconscious mind.

One way to do this is to cut pictures from magazines, books, or newspapers. Photographers have taken many wonderful professional photos that have been published in lovely form in popular periodicals. Fashion magazines tend to have more pictures that depict life situations. These are virtual fonts of manifesting fodder. The Sherlock Holmes in you will hunt out and decipher the most effective and lucrative sources. It is really fun and very insightful.

Once you have decided upon your intention, leaf through these magazines until a picture strikes you that somehow embodies the essence of your intention. It must speak to you on a higher level and you should feel empowered by looking at it. For instance, if romantic love is what you want, cut out pictures of beautiful couples holding hands, walking together, in affectionate positions, in locations that appeal to you such as the beach, a city street, or a countryside. The photos should make you feel good while looking at them so that they'll inspire you to draw a similar situation into your life. Of course, we couldn't expect or try to manifest Cindy Crawford, for heaven's sake. It's the pose she's in that is important for our purposes. You get the idea.

Let us say that you want to draw a new job or perfect career into your life. Cut out shots of men and women in business attire going to work. Professional magazines are loaded with them. A new home is your wish? Women's and interior design magazines and real estate sections of the newspaper are your source. Be creative.

You don't need a lot of pictures, even one will do. Some folks are artistic sorts and create gorgeous collages. It's not necessary. You simply need the external visual to help motivate the internal one. One of my clients set out to find a husband. In addition to her affirmations, she began collecting pictures of couples and pasting them in a notebook. She told me that each day she would look at the pictures, go into meditation, and then begin to visualize herself in those positions with a wonderful loving man. Although she couldn't clearly see the face of the gentleman, she could feel his love.

One day, overjoyed, she walked into my office and showed me her book. The pictures were very effective. Laughing, she asked me to take a good look at the feet of the male model in one of the pictures. I saw that he was wearing cowboy boots. She giggled as she told me that she had met the man of her dreams, and that he always wears cowboy boots. Now this is unusual, since we live in upstate New York! She and those pictures did some pretty fancy footwork, partner (if you pardon the pun!)—I had the pleasure of officiating at their marriage less than one year later.

You can also use personal photographs and get the same effect as magazine photos. Perhaps you are actually in the photo and would like the situation to repeat itself, or for a similar one to occur. There is a danger when using your own pictures. You must be careful not to try to manipulate someone. You can't get your boyfriend, Bob, back by using his picture. That would be a cosmic no-no and could result in very heavy karma. It is definitely not appropriate to use images to manipulate another. But if you have a photo of a former country home, you could use that shot to manifest a return visit there, to manifest repairs to the home, or to attract a new one to replace it, if you are ready to sell. You could also use that photo if you wished to manifest an entirely new vacation, as long as your intention and affirmation reflect that this is a symbol of what you want.

When using people in photographs, my strongest and most helpful advice is to use strangers in magazines. Anonymity will prevent you from getting off track or from becoming too emotional, if you are suddenly flooded with memories. You will not be tempted to manipulate or sway another if you cannot recognize the people in the pictures.

External images are used to condition your mind to receive your desire. They are springboards, nothing more. Many traditional religions have holy pictures and cards with sacred images on them. Followers are encouraged to pray while gazing at them, making a bequest of God or the saint pictured. Scrying into a crystal ball, mirror, or the ocean are all ways to induce the imaging ability of our psychic mind. I'll explain more about external influences in the next chapter. For now, here is a step-by-step method for using photographs to strengthen your visualization.

Exercise 14: Using Photos in Visualization

- Put the picture in front of you before you begin your meditation. Gaze at it and relax.

- Begin your breathing and go into your meditation. Use the scenario in the photo to start your detailed visualization.

- Jump into the picture in your mind's eye when you transfer it to your meditation and visualization. Become the person in the picture who represents you, and feel the joy and all of the emotions of the moment.

- Let your mind take it from there, and proceed with the visualization meditation as I outlined it, step by step. Let your mind flow and take over. Then continue and complete the exercise.

Viewing external pictures is just an aid to help you jump-start your own visualizing. If you use external images, you will have given your materializing power a definite boost.

It's All in Clear View

Congratulations! You have just completed the most important part of the manifesting ritual. When you look into the face of what you truly want in meditation, and then declare it, you summon the greatest powers in the Universe, which have been within you all along. Focused energy is irresistible, magnetic, and presents an unmistakable clear view of what you want to the Universe, which gets results. People and situations are literally manipulated by the force of one strong energy over the other. Therefore, the intention must always be pure and in everyone's best interest.

Think of the focus of your energy each day. Opening a stubborn jar lid, lifting a heavy object, and closing a door, for that matter, are all simple ways in which we manipulate physical energy with physical energy. The important difference here is that when we are working on manifesting, we are manipulating physical energy with mental/spiritual energy, as in a demonstration of mind over matter.

In chapter 6, we will learn to use our visions in conjunction with other symbols, objects, and tools to send our message straight to the realm where it will be accepted and subsequently propelled into our physical world. We will accomplish it without wasting an iota of our dynamic force.

When we study and learn to employ our mind power, we realize how scientific it truly is, rather than the hocus-pocus, trickster magic that many people condemn. Ours is a spiritual magic that happens when we allow the might, strength, and love within us to motivate our lives.

CHAPTER 6

Getting It Out There

*I*n manifesting, it is important to let the Universe know precisely what we want by making every effort to transmit our intention accurately. It is also crucial to give the desire as much momentum as we can by infusing it with energy. A spacecraft cannot get off the ground without sufficient fuel, the impetus that drives the vehicle forward. In our efforts to get everything we ever wanted, we must fire up our intention with the fuel of the Universe, our personal energy or thought power. External elements in our world can augment our energy, forming the perfect combination of psychic fuel. Everything that exists has energy. Multiply this energy by using various complementary elements, add it to our own physical, mental, and spiritual energy, and the Universe cannot ignore it.

It is time to focus on the ways to ensure that our requests are transmitted as powerfully as possible to the Universe. Other energies exist in our lives in order to assist us. Spirit encourages the intermingling of these forces to affect our physical world. If we make the correct choices and use the appropriate tools, we can send our message into action faster and more efficiently.

This chapter focuses on the final step in our method, *Send It*. We will learn to employ all the available instruments and rituals to draw what we desire to us. You have already performed the most difficult tasks of manifesting in the *Say It* and *See It* steps, and now you will send your intention forward and enhance it by using your individual style and creativity.

Your Personal Manifesting Style

All of us enjoy putting our own slant on the things we say and do. We develop our own individual way of dressing, writing, eating, decorating, and fixing our hair that indicate to others and the world at large who we are (or should I say, who we think we are), or who we'd like to be. This need we all have to let the world know our distinct selves is a tremendous asset to the process of manifesting. We can use the very special part of ourselves that is different from everyone else as we attempt to draw our desires into our lives.

I can hear you saying, "What style? What's so special about me?" Over and over again, my students and clients lament that there is nothing distinct about them. What a pity, if we cannot recognize or value the unique gifts given to us by God. My response to those who voice the above confusion is, "So, what's *not* special about you?" They have a tougher time answering that one once they begin to think about their abilities and talents.

Here is a brain-teasing exercise that will help you to see yourself in a special way. Think of three facts about you that others may not be aware of, and are not general knowledge about you, and write them down. This is not as easy as it seems because you are looking for things that are not obvious to others. For instance, very few people know that I paint abstract art, have a vintage hat collection, and love to dance. These may not seem monumental, but they are very significant. Their value lies in what these interests say about me as a person. In other words, what do these pursuits tell you about the kind of life I live and pleasures I seek? I will do the analysis for you.

First, I paint abstract art. This is a clue as to the way I see life: not structured or linear but spontaneous, colorful, and full of surprises. Upon reflection, I can see how this is true for me. I prefer life to be challenging, unpredictable, and exciting. Routine makes me nuts! I dislike doing the same thing twice, and a nine-to-five schedule is the death of me. I gotta be free!

Second, I have a vintage hat collection. I started this hobby about ten years ago. The fascination for me is the history of the pieces and the visual images they evoke in my imagination. Whenever I see a beautiful hat, I imagine who wore it first, what he or she was like, how much their taste mirrors mine, the art in the workmanship of the piece, whose energy, design, and love created it, and so on. I am drawn into the hat as though it were a painting, unleashing my imagination on a very personal level, since it is an article of clothing.

When I reflect upon this interest, I realize much about myself and how I relate to other folks. I understand that I am a people person, fascinated by the lure of beautiful objects and accouterments that are a part of the way people value themselves and of the quality of life they live.

Third, I love to dance. Unless you have been out boogying with me, you would not know this. All types of dance draw my eye and attention. I love to watch the graceful movements of exquisite ballerinas, the freeform style of contemporary jazz dance, and good old-fashioned tap dancing makes me want to get up and join right in! This love is reflected in my personality in many ways. My energy is always up and ready to go, waiting for my cue, I guess. I am very flexible in my thinking, and accepting of differences in myself and others, and my sense of artistic appreciation is great. Watching beautiful movement helps me to move gracefully through my life, flowing with the Universe.

It is time for you to try this exercise yourself. On the lines below or in your journal, record the three distinguishing facts about yourself that others are not likely to know about. Then record your reflections. How does this interest, pursuit, or hobby demonstrate itself in the way you see life and other people?

Be as honest as you can with yourself; this is an important exercise in self-reflection and understanding. To develop a personal manifesting style, you will need to know as much about your motivations as you can.

Exercise 15: Thoughts of You

State your three personal facts:

Fact 1: _____

Fact 2: _____

Fact 3: _____

Now, record your reflections on each of them:

Reflections on fact 1:

_____

_____

_____

_____

_____

_____

_____

_____

_____

_____

_____

Reflections on fact 2:

_____

_____

_____

_____

_____

_____

_____

_____

_____

Reflections on fact 3:

_____

_____

_____

_____

_____

_____

_____

_____

_____

I am sure you have learned some interesting details about how you see your life, as reflected in those individual facts about yourself. We will now take that information and use it to help you develop your own personal manifesting style.

Your Unique Ritual

A very interesting and fun activity of manifesting is creating a ritual that is distinctively your own. A ritual is simply an established pattern of behavior performed in a set manner. Religious rites employ rituals in weekly practices such as the Catholic Mass, Protestant services, and the rites of Earth religions around the world. Establishing a ritual that reflects yourself adds energy to your intentions and sends a clear message to the Universe. That's what this *Send It* method is all about.

Let us use an example from my responses to the exercise above. I have incorporated my love for hat collecting into my manifesting ritual. No, I don't wear a hat every time I do it, although that would be just fine, if it reflects who you are. It is the underlying essence of my reflection that I use. I stated that I feel a strong connection to objects with a history, that help me to feel my closeness to others on the planet. So I use objects in my ritual that symbolize this connection, such as a totem bear connecting me to animals, a crystal given to me by a dear friend, and trinkets from my childhood that make me feel one with the joy of youth. In addition to these, I employ my love of dance by reciting prayers and affirmations that flow into my manifesting requests beautifully. I play meditation music or nature sounds, which calm me and lift my spirits. Color is all around me in my manifesting room, demonstrating my spontaneity and love of the unusual.

You see, when we create a ritual we create a sacred space and practice that is unique to us alone. That means that we will use the same procedure every time we wish to send a request to the Universe. It is important to repeat the ritual in the same way, using the same objects, because the energy generated through the repetition gets stronger and stronger with time. If we make constant changes to our ritual or objects, we dissipate energy, thereby weakening it so the message takes longer to reach its mark.

This practice of ritual is complemented by the items you choose to include within it. These objects should echo your style, loves, interests, and desires.

They, too, will increase the momentum of energy, boosting your message and launching it into reality.

Your Place

Before we get into the specifics of choosing and using your ritual objects, you will need a space that will hold them. I use an altar.

Many of you, I am sure, are already familiar with designating a special space in which to pray, meditate, or just to be alone to reflect. There are two considerations here. First, this sacred space should not be easily accessible to others who live with you, and second, it should be permanently dedicated for your purpose. In other words, you always do your work in the same place. You can use any surface you like. In my office, I use an antique table given to my family by a dear uncle who has now passed on. At home, my altar is a dresser top. Others I know have used a shelf, bookcase, even a church pew they inherited. You can make a space on the floor for your altar, if you like—whatever is comfortable, just be consistent. Always use the same surface and place in your home. Once you have engendered and empowered your altar, any disturbance could scatter your energy and delay your manifesting. Moving your altar around the house upsets the balance of energy and slows your progress.

Getting what you want requires psychic common sense, and that requires using your head. It makes sense that if Fido or Tabby jump on your altar, their energies will disturb the calm and peace there. Yes, our beloved pets are loving and gentle, but they possess their own energies and can draw some power away from your manifesting.

Humans need to steer clear of your altar, too. You may keep your altar in sight if you live with others, as long as they understand that they cannot touch anything on it. Another way to safeguard your altar is to keep all the related items in a special box and set them up only when you are doing your ritual. You can then remove them from sight when your ritual is complete. Granted, this is a pain in the neck, but necessary if you live in a large, active household, or you simply don't want anyone to know what you are doing! Not everyone is sympathetic, and some may think you have lost your marbles. Anyway, if you choose this method, make sure you set up your items on the same surface each time. Don't jump from bed to dresser to floor to window sill, but rather choose one as the sacred space. There are so many options. Be creative!

Speaking of creativity, I have a client who uses a wooden crate. She stores all her ritual items in it and, when it's time to perform her intentions, she simply flips the crate over, covers it with a special cloth, sets up her items, and uses it as her altar. When she's done, she stores everything right in the crate and slides it under her bed. Rather clever, don't you think?

Whatever you choose, make it stick. Use the same basic items that reflect you, on the same altar, in the same place. You may, however, add objects to your altar from time to time that represent specific desires. For example, if you are trying to manifest money, you may place a dollar bill or several coins in the center of the altar to boost the money energy. If you do this, remember to remove the specific objects when you change your intention. So, after you have received your money and want to manifest a new love, remove the coins and replace them with some object that represents love to you. *Don't mix the energies.*

Once you have decided on a space for your manifesting, you can begin to consider the ritual objects you would like to use to further focus your energy.

Objects of Your Affection

The ritual items you may use are as endless and unlimited as your imagination. Choose them wisely, because they will represent your power and strength. The following is a list of basic ritual objects that have been most helpful to my own manifesting and to that of my students.

- Crystals and stones
- Trinkets

- Coins

- Photographs

- Jewelry

- Religious statues and icons

- Items representing the four elements of the Universe:

    Water: A cup of water

    Earth: A bowl of sand or soil from a garden, a plant,
    or fresh flowers

    Air: Incense

    Fire: Candles

You should choose basic objects that will remain in your sacred space or on your altar, and vary the additional items that reflect your specific intention. I have had clients use doll clothing when trying to manifest a new wardrobe. It worked! As long as the object has meaning *for you*, it will be effective. Let's take a look at a typical altar with its basic objects.

An altar is a very personal thing. It needs to be comfortable and significant to you, and it should express your style. I have a love of things oriental, so my altar demonstrates that: Chinese bowls and a Japanese Zen fountain adorn it. The fountain is soothing as well as reflective of my love of the sea. My sacred space sports a large quartz crystal, a large amethyst crystal, a large wand encrusted with stones that represent the seven energy centers of the body (or chakras), and five candles in holders. I also have a small bowl filled with soil from my former home in Georgia. The bowl was made by American Cherokee Indians and given to me by a close friend. A brass incense burner and assorted totems also grace my altar, including bears and dolphins of stone and wood, as well as a precious statue of the Buddha. All of the universal elements— earth, fire, air and water—are represented, because I feel they have the power to focus my spiritual energy and help me create my physical world.

Your altar need not be as elaborate as mine. A single candle will do. Remember it is up to you. Your intention will be heard and answered by Spirit whether you have one object or ten. The whole point of having the sacred space is simply to direct your energy. I offer these options for those of us who like reminders and are comfortable and inspired by visual representations.

To help you choose your objects, I'll give you some insights into the ones I listed earlier and how they can help you draw your desires to you.

Crystals and Stones

It is no surprise that crystals, formed in the Earth, generate energy. Just think about that when you look down at the quartz-driven watch you are wearing! For centuries, we have known the power of crystals. On the ancient continent of Atlantis, crystals were said to be the prime source of power, not only running primitive machinery but able to house information for later use, much like our modern-day computer chip. When you hold a crystal that is alive and well, you will feel a pulsating movement or a tingling in your hand. Sometimes, depending upon how powerful the crystal is, the feeling will travel up your arm or throughout your entire body. These are said to be healthy crystals and are perfect for humans to adopt and use in rituals.

Some crystals have been mistreated and abused. An unhealthy crystal is one that might have been dropped or kept in a dark place for an extended amount of time (crystals need sunlight and moonlight to recharge once they have been removed from the Earth) or some negative person might have been in possession of it or in its vicinity. Such crystals have lost some energy and may not work for you.

When shopping for a crystal to assist in your manifesting, it is wise to go to a store that has a pleasing sense about it—you know, the kind of place where you feel comfortable. If the shop is off-putting, leave. Chances are the energy in the whole place is negative. One important thing to know about crystals is they will pick up on the energy around them, absorb it, and project it. You don't want any negativity poisoning your intention, so be careful. If a dear friend gives you a crystal as a gift, and note I said *dear* friend, it should be fine. Never take a crystal from a stranger or someone you don't know well, even if they seem very nice. You don't know enough about them or where that specific piece came from in the first place. Your safest bet is to pick your own.

Crystals are said to have powers related to specific intentions. Any good book on crystals and their particular properties will help you to select the perfect one for your intention (see the bibliography in this book for my favorite volumes). For instance, if you want to draw love into your life, a rose quartz crystal is best. If you want to open up to your spiritual self or draw in divine energy, a purple amethyst will do the trick. Do a little research if you like the idea of using crystals and stones, and then make your choice accordingly.

The same information applies to stones. Stones are simply more dense than crystals and form closer to the surface of the Earth. Crystals form below the surface of the Earth, deep in its caverns. One easy way to recognize crystals, as opposed to stones, is that crystals are clear and can be transparent. They look like colored glass. Stones are opaque and you can't see through them. You might have heard the names of some stones, such as obsidian, onyx, turquoise, agate, etc. Even precious stones are great for manifesting, such as ruby, diamond, emerald, sapphire, etc. You can wear crystals, stones, and precious stones in jewelry form. So after you've done your ritual, you can then wear the stone that has been on the altar and carry the energy with you.

If you have done your homework and know what crystal or stone you are looking for, allow your eye to make the first choice. Usually the available stock will be displayed in a bowl of some sort. Look through the pile of stones in the bowl until you see one that attracts you. Put it in one of your palms and close your hand over it. If you feel some pulsing or tingling, it's yours. If you feel nothing, shift hands and try the process again (one hand may be more sensitive than the other.) Still don't sense anything? Try holding the crystal or stone with your fingertips instead of your palm. No luck? Then put it back and try another one. Remember, crystals can loose their spark so keep trying until you get a live one!

Some people never feel anything when holding crystals or stones. That is not a problem. The piece will still work for you. You are just one of those folks who are not sensitive to crystal or stone vibrations—yet. Give it time. Eventually, you will become more sensitive to them. For now, choose your stones by sight.

Trinkets

Trinkets are a lot simpler to choose than crystals or stones. Anything you are attracted to will do. Some pieces that might work are medals, talismans, buttons, pins, or ribbons. I have used bark that had fallen from a special tree I love. It is never spiritually appropriate to harm a living plant for manifesting purposes. Make sure that the item has already been discarded by the plant itself, like a fallen branch or a leaf. You and the tree or plant will be a lot happier, and definitely in harmony with each other.

You can use anything that applies to your intention. If you are trying to draw love into your life, you could use a small Cupid pendant or a heart-shaped button, anything that reminds you of your essence. Place your choices on your altar in a bowl, an open box, or jar, or just lay them there. They will help to focus your energy.

Coins or Bills

In manifesting rituals to draw money, I always use some coins. Dimes, nickels, pennies, quarters, half-dollars, silver dollars, or even gold coins will be fine. You can also include paper money, too. Here is a tip: if you wish, you can substitute fake or play money for the real thing. It works just as well.

Photographs

Those photographs you so skillfully selected and used in your visualization in chapter 5 will come in handy now. Take the photos or magazine cutouts and put them on your altar. Nothing to it. Place them so that you can easily see them. You'll still need to use them to induce your visualization. The process requires you to *See It* before you *Send It*.

Jewelry

In addition to using your crystal or stones in jewelry form, you can actually use a piece of precious jewelry, gold, or silver to assist in the manifesting process. Wearing the item while you are waiting for your intention to materialize keeps the energy with you at all times. It is harmless to your intention if you remove the jewelry from the altar or sacred space because you are not dissipating the energy. You are enhancing it by keeping the symbol with you at all times. What you *cannot* do is put back the jewelry into your jewelry box! You'll need to keep it with the other ritual items or wear it until the request comes to pass.

The precious metals of silver and gold have long been used for sacred rites and ceremonies, and are said to embody the powerful energies existent within the sun and moon. Gold is said to enhance with the fire of the sun. Silver is said to calm with the coolness of the moon. You can find more about the spiritual properties of precious metals in the same books that cover the crystals and stones.

Religious Statues and Icons

In order to invoke a sense of the Universe, I find it comforting to use a representation of God/the Source in my manifesting. If there is a particular religious creed you adhere to, or if you are fond of a specific persona within it, you may use that statue or icon on your altar. Many people use statues of Jesus, the Virgin Mary, St. Francis, and other Christian symbols. If your philosophy is Eastern in nature, statues of the Buddha, Mohammed, Shiva, etc., may be used as well. If you practice Earth religions, a pentacle or Goddess statue will work. Pictures of these deities will be just as effective. I always have one or more of these on my altar. It does not matter how diverse they are—remember, you are looking for a symbol of what God means to you. Place it anywhere that is comfortable to oversee your work, so to speak.

Items Representing the Four Elements of the Universe

Symbols of the four elements of the Universe would be essential on the altar of anyone who feels close to nature or Mother Earth. American Indians in particular feel strong connections to these symbols. I tend to use them because they give me a sense of completeness. They make me feel at one with my physical existence.

For our purposes, it does not matter where you place these elements, but earth religions and American Indian tradition place them in the four geographical directions: Water—West; Fire—East; Earth—North; Air—South. Unless your religion specifies, I have found that just the presence of these elements on my altar is enough, so don't be alarmed if they are not in the correct position. Use your intuition to decide where to put them. Here is what they represent:

A cup of water: the sea, the source of our beginning, and the flow of life

A bowl of sand or soil from a garden, a plant, or fresh flowers: the Earth, our Mother, our home in this lifetime

Incense: the air, the life force, our breath

Candles: fire, the energy that drives us forward

Candles are unique unto themselves. A whole chapter can be devoted to the use of candles, and many entire books have been. I always use white candles because they are neutral. Colors represent energy vibrations, so it is best to use white, which encompasses all the colors in the spectrum. You can get very specific with candle colors whose vibrations match your intentions, if you like (see suggestions in the bibliography should you choose to go into depth with candle colors and meanings). Getting specific with candles is wonderful, but believe me, you can still get results that are just as effective with a simple white candle. In fact, even if you choose not to use all the elements, always use a candle. I would never do a ritual without one. Humans have been petitioning the Universe and praying with them for eons. The hypnotic flame can relax you and can quickly put you into alpha state, where your message takes flight.

Arrange the objects on your altar as you see fit. Interact with them during your ritual, if you like, by focusing your intention on them or touching them. The following is a sample ritual that might be used.

Exercise 16: Sample Ritual Using Your Altar and Accouterments

1. Set up your altar and turn on some appropriate, soothing music or Earth sounds (optional).

2. Arrange your objects, bless, and thank them for helping you get what you desire. This consecrates or "charges" them with energy to enhance your purpose.

3. Place your written intention on the altar so that it is in an easily readable position.

4. Sit, stand, or kneel before your altar.

5. Before you begin your ritual, ask the Universe/God/Goddess/All There Is to put a circle of white light of love and protection around you and your altar. This will ensure that you are drawing the highest possible good to you and your work.

6. Light your candle(s) and incense.

7. Say your affirmation/intention out loud. You might choose to hold a stone or crystal while you voice your written affirmation and intention. It can be comforting and the stone's vibration can put you into a calmer, more relaxed trance state.

8. Relax and begin your visualization meditation.

9. When you feel your visualization is complete, say a prayer of your choice (optional) and words of thanks, adding the gratitude part of the affirmation.

10. Stay in silent meditation for a moment.

11. When you come out of meditation, take a deep breath and return to full consciousness.

12. Allow your candle to burn, if you like, until it burns itself out. Do this only if you will be staying at home. Otherwise, extinguish the candle by snuffing it. Blowing it out dissipates the energy. You may use the same candle the next time you do your ritual, but only for the same specific intention. Don't use this candle if you are switching intentions, for example, from love to money, because it will confuse the message. Throw it out when your intention manifests in physical form, and use a new one for each new intention.

All of the above objects are acceptable, if you choose to add them to your ritual. I must emphasize that you have the option of being as elaborate or as simple as you wish. All of these objects *enhance. They do not do the work for you.* The only way to draw what you want into your life is to have a clear focus and a pure intention. Everything else can be stripped away and you will still be able to change your life for the better.

It is important not to become too dependent on any objects. Look at them as additions to your ritual, not absolute necessities. The power to manifest lies within you, not in an object. Only you, your thoughts, and your energy can impact your future.

More Questions

At this point, I'm sure several questions arise. "How often shall I do this ritual?" "How long does it take?" "When will I get what I want?" "May I do more than one ritual in a day?" "May I combine intentions at the same ritual, if they are related?" Here are your answers:

How often shall I do this ritual?

Like everything else, the number of times you repeat your ritual is up to you. You may do it every day, if you feel you need reinforcing to stay focused. The Universe only needs to hear your intention once. The repetition is for us. We humans need to know we have made our point in the most powerful way possible. Personally, I do my ritual according to the duration of the candle. If I use a taper candle, I do a ritual and burn it for an hour each day until it burns out. I have also divided my ritual in thirds, doing it for three days straight, dividing my candle into three burning sessions. Three and multiples of three are said to be sacred numbers, further supporting the request.

You can do your ritual once, allow your candle to burn itself out at that session, and not repeat it again. If you do this, you must still say your affirmation each day until the intention materializes in your life. That is necessary when you begin this work. When you become more experienced at focusing your energy, you need only perform one ritual per intention and repeat your affirmation using your intuitive sense to guide you. In other words, when you feel it is enough, it is.

How long does it take?

A ritual can take anywhere from five to thirty minutes, depending on how long you do the meditation visualization and the closing meditation. This, again, is up to the individual.

When will I get what I want?

This question goes back to something I mentioned earlier in the book. You will receive your request when it is right and perfect to do so. The Universe has to get all the elements to come together, and that takes time. Offer your intention, and be ready to wait. I have known my intentions to be manifest in a minute, an hour, a day, a week, a month, or a year. That part is in the hands of the Universe. Be patient and know that you have been heard, and trust that your request will be satisfied.

May I do more than one ritual in a day?

No. This will only confuse you and your energy, and will send mixed messages to the Universe. Prioritize. Decide what you want first, and work on that for a while. Once you have seen results, you can switch to another intention. But never do more than one ritual in a day, even if it is for the same intention. Wait twenty-four hours. If you are too anxious, you send the message that you are trying to control the Universe, and could stop the process dead in its tracks.

May I combine intentions at the same ritual, if they are related?

No, again. The same rules as above apply.

A Fitting Sendoff

You have now used the power within you to enable your desire to reach the Universe. Your mind, thoughts, willpower, and inner strength are at work here. The God within you is more than capable of sending you what you want and need. The rest is up to you. Do your half. Repeat your affirmation every day. Carry your intention in the form of a positive attitude into your daily life. Expect that what you want is on its way. Don't ever lose hope. Live in preparation for what you have requested, so that when it arrives you are ready for it. The forces in Spirit are working for you as long as you expect success. You will be a magnet for synchronistic events. Each day, your desires will begin to unfold in your life. Be patient. All of the elements are coming together for you. Wait, be positive, keep believing, and all will surely be yours.

Here is a final comforting thought. You are not alone. There are other energies in Spirit, loving entities, waiting for you to call upon them. They exist to help you. The next chapter will introduce them to you, and show you ways to draw celestial energies into your manifesting.

CHAPTER 7

Getting Inside and Outside Help

*T*he term "the Universe" can often seem lofty and somehow distant to us everyday folks down here on the Earth. When we think of the Universe, we imagine the darkness of space with stars, moons, planets, and an occasional meteor. We envision the science fiction movies of our youth and not a deity, a tremendous energy force, working for our greater good. We must adjust our thinking and accept that there are other available sources within our Universe waiting to assist us in manifesting our desires.

The Universe, as we interpret it, encompasses all energies that exist, period—all of them, those existing in physical form and those existing in spirit form. We can see some energies with our physical eyes, since they consist of matter. But there are many energies we cannot see that are ready to assist us in making the quality of our lives the best it can be.

The celestial energies I'm speaking of are not to be feared. They are loving spirits dedicated to helping us achieve all that we desire. Scientists tell us that energy doesn't die, it is constant. It exists simultaneously with us on another plane of reality that we cannot necessarily see, and that plane can interact with us. Spiritually, we know that this interaction can take place by focusing the mind. Energy is generated by thoughts, which can alter physical reality. The metaphysical perspective teaches that this unseen energy is essentially a thought form created within the human psyche. This energy is part of us, generated by us, and a function of the source we call God.

The idea that there are benevolent forces that exist to provide human beings with comfort, help, guidance, support, and protection is not a new one. Most of the Earth's major religions believe that the soul lives on after physical death, and that we can receive guidance from this realm. Many religious traditions recognize saints, angels, and sacred spirits, such as the Holy Ghost.

For example, there are many accounts in the Bible that speak of angelic visitations. Angels are said to have appeared to the Virgin Mary, her mother, and countless others. Angels have played a tremendous role in the belief system of Christianity, but these communications appear to be reserved for "special" people, those with a distinct mission from God. But, in truth, we are all on a sacred mission from God. Our lives all have meaning, and we were born for a reason—to serve God and our fellow man. It follows, then, that if God exists within us, all around us, and in all things, that we can have direct access to It. If we can access God, surely we can access Its creations that exist as spirits. Not only do these energies exist, but anyone can communicate with them.

Over the years, we have seen and heard of many psychics and mediums who have made contact with celestial energies with uncanny accuracy. George Anderson, an interesting and remarkably accurate medium, is a devout Catholic who shares his gifts joyfully, as he lives his own mission from God. Medium James Van Praagh, author of the book *Talking To Heaven*, has demonstrated to millions in television audiences his prowess at communicating with the beyond. The messages that come back to us through these two mediums are mostly consoling, but sometimes contain warnings to prevent calamity. I could name many, many others who do this work, including myself. The one overarching point is that this type of liaison exists, and it does so to help us. What other reason would angels or our loved ones have to communicate in such a way?

The idea that some maleficent force exists that wants to hurt us—the devil, for example—is totally relative to your beliefs. In my New Thought church we are taught that there is only positive or negative energy, all generated by us. So if you believe the devil exists, it does. To the contrary, if you believe as I do that negativity exists in the Universe but is powerless against love, you have nothing to fear. The evil spirits some speak of are, in fact, thought forms, given impetus and energy by the people who believe in them. What do you believe?

Only loving energy will come to you when you pray, affirm, and summon it. We protect ourselves with our white circle of light when we manifest, in order to reinforce our own belief that God is within and all around us, caring for us and keeping negativity in the form of our own thoughts, fears, and doubts at bay. Within this context of positive energy, affirmation, and prayer, we can open our hearts and minds to those forces waiting to lend us a helping hand.

Lions and Tigers and Bears, Oh My!

Well, maybe not *quite* lions, tigers, and bears. In the *Wizard Of Oz*, Dorothy and her friends are on the constant lookout for ominous beings who mean them no good. Yet they are consistently helped in their travels by those who wish them well, like Glenda the Good Witch, the Munchkins, and the citizens of Emerald City.

We humans, as we follow our own yellow brick road, meet with perils and pals. As Dorothy, the Tin Man, and the Cowardly Lion came to understand, the power to make our dreams come true lies within us. But along the way we, too, need to rely on the love and generosity of others. This guidance is not limited to those beings we can see, but extends to a greater consciousness that includes energies known as angels, spirit guides, and our loved ones who have passed into spirit.

Hello, Is Anybody There?

They are there, all right. The means that spiritual energies use to communicate with us is our own mind. These loving messengers guide us in many ways. We could experience intuitive urgings that seem like our own thoughts at first but, upon reflection, we realize it couldn't possibly be us. We might hear a word or phrase in our mind's ear prompting us to do or not to do something.

A friend of mine who lived in Manhattan often strolled unafraid along the streets of her relatively safe Chelsea. One day, on one of her walks, she reached a familiar corner where she often crossed the street to return to her apartment. As she began to step into the crosswalk, she heard a resounding "voice" in her head. She described the voice as definitely not her own. It was yelling at her with some enthusiasm, and shouting, "Don't cross now. Don't cross the street!" Alarmed at this, my friend stopped dead in her tracks, remaining on the corner sidewalk. Within seconds, two men with pistols ran out of the deli located exactly on the opposite corner. My friend would have crossed directly in front of that store, had she proceeded. These robbers were shooting as they emerged and wounded several unfortunate, innocent bystanders who happened to be in their line of fire. Watching from the relative safety of the other side of the street, my friend witnessed this event with horror. Had she crossed, she surely would have been in grave danger, if not killed. The "voice" knew what was to transpire and warned her as best it could. Thank God!

Events such as this one are not unusual. If we are not receiving inside help, prompting thoughts or discarnate "voices" in our minds, we are receiving outside help from energies that can literally transmute into any form in our physical world.

Another friend told me of an experience she had in which her life was literally saved by a loving energy. She was on her way to visit a friend one evening and was looking for a convenient place to park her car. Unfortunately, none were available, so she was forced to park on a very steep hill. There were no cars parked behind hers, other drivers apparently not taking the chance.

As she got out of the car, it somehow slipped out of gear and began to roll backward, down the hill. The door was open and knocked her over as she attempted to get back in the vehicle to stop it. My friend is very tall and slim, and the weight of the car, as it rolled, wedged her legs under the door and began dragging her down the hill. She remembers the excruciating pain as she was pulled along rocks and dirt in the street, her legs crushed under the door. No one was there on the street that night as she called for help.

She told me that when she was knocked over, her head hit the pavement and she blacked out. Right before losing consciousness, she asked God for help. The next thing she remembers is hearing a gentle voice tell her that all would be well. Then she saw a tremendously bright, white light all around her, and felt her entire body being lifted and "flown" above the car. When she awoke, she was lying on the grass next to the car, paralyzed. Unable to move, she waited about an hour until someone saw her and called an ambulance.

The light remained with her, reassuring her that she would be fine. She was hurt very seriously and in critical condition for months, drifting in and out of consciousness but somehow knowing that she would be healed. The doctors did not give her a good prognosis. She was told that she would not be able to walk again. Her parents prayed for her healing and promised that, if God healed her, they would devote their lives to His work. Needless to say, my friend was completely healed, and her parents are ordained ministers today.

Angels Among Us

Many people have told astounding stories of the intervention of angels in the lives of ordinary humans. In some cases, angels have appeared in the form of people or animals who arrive just in the nick of time to save someone from terrible circumstances, as they did to my friend in the story above. In the last ten years or so, many accounts of angelic interventions have been recorded in books, magazines, and on television shows. More people in our society today are said to believe in the existence of angels than ever before.

Angels have the power to save our lives and protect our physical bodies. In reality they are just energy, with no real form at all. They may appear to us in our mind's eye in meditation or as apparitions viewed with the physical eyes. They have been reported to appear to people in human form, with or without wings, as ethereal, gossamer-like transparent forms, or even pinpoints of light.

Messengers of Light, as angels have sometimes been called, can appear as humans of any racial or ethnic origin. They can take male or female form, since they have no assigned gender. An angel will reveal itself to someone in the gender that is most comfortable for that individual. Whatever form they take, angels can and do make themselves known to us mortals, from time to time.

There is absolutely no doubt in my mind that angels exist. I have been most fortunate in that I have had an angel intervene in my life to protect me. From that day on, my life changed for the better.

The Good Shepherd

About seven years ago, I was an actress and director working in New York City. One morning at about seven o'clock I was driving my car into Manhattan, on my way to work on a new film. When I reached the West Side Highway, one of the busiest in New York City, my car began to smoke and stopped dead in the middle of the entrance ramp. It was rush hour, so I tied up traffic for miles, much to the dismay of motorists trying to get on the highway. There was nothing I could do. Eventually, a police car pulled up and the two officers pushed my car off the ramp onto a service road in one of the more dangerous neighborhoods in the city, and left me there. They assured me that they would call a service station and help would be on the way.

Unfortunately, I had to wait—a woman alone in this questionable, deserted place. It was a stereotypical New York street, complete with trash, broken glass, and graffiti. Needless to say, I was more than a little afraid. I tried to calm myself when, after thirty minutes, help was nowhere to be found. It is notoriously unsafe for anyone, especially a woman, to walk alone in a bad neighborhood in New York City any time of the day, let alone the desolate early morning hours, so I resolved to just sit and pray.

I asked God to help me out. I told God I was afraid and needed protection. As I finished my prayer, I turned to my left to see, standing next to my car and looking peacefully in the window, the most beautiful German shepherd dog I had ever seen. He was huge. I'm normally afraid of large dogs but something, perhaps the kindness in his big brown eyes, persuaded me to open my window to pet him. When I lowered it, my friend rested his muzzle on the window's ledge to receive my caress. I realized that he was standing in the street and could be hit by a passing car, so I spoke to him. I told him to come around to the other side of the car, onto the sidewalk, so he wouldn't get hurt. As if understanding my every word, he followed my instruction. I climbed over the console in my car to sit on the passenger side, and bravely opened the door. This gentle giant lay down next to me on piles of cracked glass and debris as I petted him and thanked him for being with me.

The dog was not visible by anyone walking toward the car on the sidewalk, since the open door blocked him from view. Within a few moments, I looked up to see two men walking toward me and my vehicle. They did not look as though they came to help, if you know what I mean. Their disheveled appearance spoke volumes, and as a gal who was born and raised in that city, I knew they meant trouble.

Obviously confused, I didn't know what to do. I was trapped by a car that wouldn't move and a large dog too big to shoo away in a hurry. It would have been impossible to usher the dog aside, close the door, and retreat into the car. And, even if I could do it, the car afforded very little protection against two large men.

As the men drew nearer to me, they obviously did not see the German shepherd. When they were within six feet of my car, the dog got up, walked around the door, and began to growl and snarl at them. Alarmed by such an unexpected scare, they did an about-face and ran away. When they were safely out of sight, my dog silently returned to my side and lay down as he had been before. I knew then that I was dealing with a very special energy.

In what seemed only moments, I heard a friendly voice call my name. Pulling up next to my car was my singing teacher, Dale, who saw my car and me being towed by the police while on his way to drop his wife off at work. He doubled back to help me. When Dale got out of his car and walked over to me, the dog made no aggressive move toward him but rather approached him as a loving friend. Dale was astonished to see the animal. I told him the story and he agreed that something bigger than all of us was happening.

The dog waited with me until Dale returned, having gone to purchase a hose to repair the engine. Dale brought food for the dog and proceeded to fix my car. The animal didn't eat the food, nor did he look underfed. His coat was shiny and beautiful. He appeared to be the picture of health and not an abandoned street animal, by any means. It was odd that he wore no collar and no tags to identify his owners.

I stood next to Dale as he fixed the car hose, and the dog stood between us, leaning on us as though he knew and loved us for years. In my panic, I realized that I had locked my keys inside the car. Dale suggested we walk to the nearest police station, several blocks away, to get help. I agreed and looked back toward the dog, but he was gone.

"He's gone! How did he get away so fast?" I blurted out. He was much too big to run that fast, and besides, we would have seen him running away. We dropped everything and looked in all directions, but he was gone—vanished.

I had read that angels can disappear at will. All I know is that without that angel-dog, my life was in grave danger. He protected me, as angels have been known to do, and when his work was done, he returned to the Love that sent him to me in the first place.

After that experience, I was convinced that all I had heard was true. Angels do exist and come to us when we need them. I am also sure that I had that experience so I could relay it to you.

Make a Date with an Angel

If you'd like to try to meet your angel, soul to soul, I offer you this meditation, given to me by my angel, Gabriel. It has worked well for my students. Don't do this exercise during a ritual. Do it at your leisure, when your focus is just on your angel, so that nothing else distracts you. Your angel might appear to you as light or a colored mist, or you might see him or her in full human form, with or without wings. Some angels have manifested themselves as symbols or patterns in the mind's eye. Whatever form they take, don't discount it.

As with all meditations, make sure you remove any fears or blocks to clear the way for accurate communication. You can easily do this by affirming,

I remove all fears and blocks to communicating with my highest angel from all levels of my consciousness. I am open, willing, and ready to receive this loving energy. God's light and protection surround me, and I am safe. And so it is!

Exercise 17: Angel Meditation

1. Relax, take three deep breaths, and enter a mild trance state.

2. As you drift slowly into meditation, clear your mind of all thoughts.

3. See, in your mind, a circle of white protective light swirling around you.

4. Focus on the words, "My Highest Angel, come to me, now." Repeat these words three times.

5. Wait, with eyes closed, until you see or perceive the presence of your angel.

6. Allow the meditation to flow, and your angel's message to come to you.

7. When the communication is complete, thank your angel for coming, and send it back to the Light.

8. Take three final deep breaths, and on the third, as you exhale, return to full consciousness.

Calling All Angels

In less than dramatic fashion, angels can be summoned to help us to get everything we desire in much the same way that they protect our bodies. You have only to ask, and your special angel will help you.

There are angels who are assigned to us by God at birth, and angels who come for special needs and requests. If you want angelic help to get your heart's desires, just add a simple affirmation to your ritual *before* you state your intention, lest you forget after your meditation. Here is the one I use:

I thank my most beloved angel for being with me today.
Thank you for helping me to receive my desire and for guiding
my path, now and throughout my life. I call all angels who are
with me to help me to receive what I ask, or something better,
in a gentle and loving way, in my greatest good. And so it is.

You couldn't have any better help than that of your angels. Call them and know that they are with you.

Spirit Guides

Among the other assistants in the Universe are energies that help us with specific day-to-day living. These forces are called our spirit guides. They are truly our best buddies on the astral plane. These beings have lived with us in other lifetimes as friends, relatives, or lovers. When we were in spirit form, before being born into this current lifetime, we made a kind of deal with another spirit that he or she would guide us from the spiritual plane, and we would live out the lifetime in physical human form. This kindred soul agreed to assist us from the astral plane throughout the lifetime. In this way, the guide furthers his or her own spiritual growth, and we both benefit from this arrangement.

Spirit guides are those entities that might have been considered guardian angels of old. Because they work so closely with us, these guides have been mistaken for angels down through the centuries, but they are really quite different from angels. They do not have the power to protect our physical bodies, other than shouting in our mind's ear to get us out of harm's way. They cannot lift or move our bodies. Neither can they transmute into any physical form, from human to animal, as angels can, nor can they appear as Light. In many cases, the voices heard by our ancestors in the Bible might have truly been these guides communicating with them.

Our spirit guides are different from our angels in that they assist us on a more mundane level. They help us to make decisions, end confusion, make choices, and guide us on our journey to the most appropriate path for our soul. The path, of course, is our spiritual journey, the road leading to our enlightenment. Guides support our highest good and try to lead us to it. Of course, angels can do all this and more, yet they tend to leave the everyday stuff to the guides.

One of the most important points about guides is that they will not tell us what to do. Their function is to offer the most harmonious options, and then sit back and allow our free will to make the choices. Psychic junkies get hooked on the mistaken idea that they no longer have to make choices once in contact with their guide—wrong. It doesn't work that way. The guides will suggest, but never coerce. They never force us to do their bidding. But they have been known to bug us until we do something, or take action.

Some of us, such as myself, are fortunate in that we are clairaudient and can hear our guides as voices in our heads. My guide has been relentless in getting me to make choices on occasion. He practically screamed to me to apply for an adjunct position teaching at a local college, which I distinctly did not want to do. I couldn't get his voice out of my head until I found myself sitting in the department chairman's office. Needless to say, I got the job, which led to an even greater opportunity to work on a local television news show. I could have ignored him, but I knew better. Besides, I had nothing to lose. The end result has brought me great joy and fulfillment.

Guides also communicate by appearing and delivering messages in our dreams. They can also write to us in a form known as automatic writing, in which we clear our mind and transcribe thoughts to paper without censorship. Upon reading such texts, we can see that the language is usually much more archaic than our own, and much wiser.

I would have to write another entire book in order to fill you in on the mysteries and wonders of spirit guides. Others have already done so. Just check the bibliography at the end of this book for my favorites. There are also classes you can take that give instruction on communicating directly with your guides. I teach these at my center. Establishing a relationship with your guide is vital to getting what you want, because engaging as much power on your side as you can makes your dreams come true faster and more efficiently.

Guides have interesting personalities and histories. In my channeling sessions, I have been privileged to introduce hundreds of people to their guides over the years. I can hear them and see them in my mind, and deliver their messages. I have channeled guides from every century, walk of life, and age group. Guides take on the personality of the lifetime in which our consciousness remembers them. In other words, they appear and deal with us in the persona that is most comfortable for our soul, not necessarily our conscious mind, to handle.

Some of the guides I have worked with have spoken in foreign languages. When this happens, I ask them to translate for the client, and they realize they must speak the colloquial language in order to do their job. A Chinese guide I once knew refused to translate, but rather decided to send pictures instead of words. It didn't matter, because the picture messages were as clear and accurate as the words would have been.

Other guides have communicated telepathically, sending thoughts so that I just "know" what they mean. They can also appear in dreams. All of these forms of communication are equally as accurate. The point is that guides are determined to communicate with us, one way or another.

Roger Who?

I met my own guide, Roger, in a most unusual way. Meeting him changed my life. Before our formal encounter (guides are with us from birth, we just don't necessarily know it), I was definitely not a spiritual seeker. I was preoccupied with my theater career and not at all interested in the ways of the Universe. At the time, I had a dear friend, Becky, who was very much involved in things supernatural, having explored it as an interest and hobby for years. She introduced me to the world of metaphysics but my interest was limited to an occasional psychic reading and the horoscope in the *New York Daily News*.

One fateful weekend evening, on a trip to the New Jersey shore, we were confined to our hotel room because of rain. Earlier that day, we had stopped in a bookstore and Becky left, as usual, with an armful of New Age books and a fortunetelling game. That game was a surprising catalyst.

As we played, I closed my eyes and began to feel faint. I was holding Becky's ring in my hand, getting ready to place it on the playing board, when my fingers locked in place around it, and it began to move in my hand, much like a Mexican jumping bean. I was terrified and started to yell. Thank God, my friend kept her head, told me to calm down, and said she thought she knew what was happening. She'd read about it. Assuring me I was fine, she urged me to close my eyes and wait. "Do you see anything?" she asked. See what?

Suddenly, I saw a movie running in my mind's eye. I told Becky about it. She was astonished when she realized I was describing someone in detail whom she knew well, but whom I had never met. I described not only his appearance, but every inch of his office, which was in Dallas, Texas. Something strange was happening.

After about thirty minutes of this, Becky asked if I could hear anything. I focused on "hearing" something in my mind, and very clearly I heard a voice say, "Hello, finally." Shaken, I asked who it was. The voice said, "Roger. Roger Smythe. I am your guide, and it's nice to meet you." Some vacation, scared half to death by a disembodied voice!

But Roger was warm, friendly, and very wise. He told me we had much work to do, and that he would be there to help me. He told me he was an actor in London, and the year in time from which he was communicating with me was 1890. We were together at the time as fellow actors and dear friends. This is how my soul chose to know him. Incidentally, I heard Roger for the first time in 1990, exactly one hundred years after we shared our life together.

From that day on, Roger has encouraged me to pursue my ministry, helping others to realize their own spirituality. Through me, he helps others find their way. It is Roger's friendly and loving support that assists me in living a joyful, spiritual life, connected to the God within me. Celestial energies that are summoned for positive purposes are loving and spiritual. They were created by the one sacred Source in the Universe that creates everything, God. Just as we are one with God, we are one with all of the energy of Its creation.

My experience is an unusual one. Most people meet their guides in a much less dramatic way. Many of my clients tell me that they know there is a presence with them, and often ask it for assistance.

Roger gave me a meditation for meeting guides. Try this as you would the angel meditation, at a time other than during your ritual. Don't try to meet both your angel and spirit guide at the same time, or on the same day. Give your energy a rest. Contact one, work with it for a week or so, and then call in the other energy. My advice is to work with your angel first, and then your guide.

Exercise 18: Spirit Guide Meditation

1. Relax, take three deep breaths, and enter a mild trance state.

2. As you drift slowly into meditation, clear your mind of all thoughts, and ask your guide to make itself known to you.

3. See, in your mind, a circle of white protective light swirling around you.

4. Feel yourself drifting to a sacred space either in nature or in a special room.

5. See it clearly before you, as it forms in your mind's eye.

6. Find a place to relax and sit down, and look straight ahead of you.

7. In a moment, as you focus, you will begin to see a figure approaching you.

8. As your guide approaches, greet him or her and thank him for coming.

9. Allow the meditation to flow, and your guide's message to come to you.

10. When the communication is complete, thank your guide for coming and send it back to the Light.

11. Take three final, deep breaths, and on the third, as you exhale, return to full consciousness.

Guiding Lights

For our purposes in manifesting, it is unnecessary to know exactly who your guide is, or what his or her name is. Of course you could pursue that using the above meditation, but it is simply enough to recognize that this energy exists to help you, and ask for its assistance. A simple affirmation is all you need. Here's one I recommend to my students:

*I thank my spirit guide for being with me today. Thank you
for helping me to receive my desire and for guiding my path,
now and throughout my life. I ask my guide, my dear friend
in spirit, to help me make harmonious choices as I open
to receiving my greatest and highest good. And so it is.*

Say this affirmation, if you wish, before beginning your visualization meditation. Here's a news flash: your guide will help you, as will your angel, even if you don't ask. Asking reassures us and focuses our intention.

Our Spiritual Family

A discussion of helping, loving energies would not be complete without the mention of our dear ones in spirit. I am speaking of our relatives and friends who have passed on or made the transition to the other side, as we metaphysicians like to say. In my work, I have had the honor of connecting loved ones on the Earth with their spiritual family. Many people have said that they continue to feel the presence of their loved one long after he or she has died. That is so because their love holds that spirit to them. Love is the tie that binds us to each other. As long as we grieve, we hold the spirit close to the Earth. The time must come when we release the spirit to move on to his or her growth on the other side. If we don't, their concern for us holds them back. They are in a much better place than we could imagine, waiting to move on to their next spiritual assignment.

Once we have released our loved ones to do their thing, they are free to assist us in drawing to us what we desire. I had a client whose mother, on the other side, told her that she was working on getting her a husband! My client laughed when she heard that and said, "She's still the same. Good, I need her help!"

As with the other entities in Spirit, our loved ones work with us by focusing their energy on our intention, if we ask them to. Because they are closer to us, having been in physical form during our lifetime, it's easier to access the spirits of our loved ones than spirit guides and angels. All we need to do is think about them, and our love draws them near. There is no great mystery to communicating with them. Just have a conversation with them, as though they were still with you. Tell them what you need or want and, quite simply, ask for their help. That's it.

You might be surprised to know that there are relatives that you have never met or known in your life who are working for you in spirit. On many occasions, my clients have received messages from great, great, great, great grandfathers, grandmothers, or ancient uncles and aunts. Some have heard from brothers and sisters who had passed on before they themselves were born. There are no limits to spirit, so anyone who loves you, whether you know them or not, can be of help to you. Cover this base by saying the following affirmation anytime you wish to contact a loved one. Find a comfortable place to sit, relax, take three gentle breaths, and begin. When you've finished the affirmation, relax and know that the one you love is now working in your highest good, across time and space.

I thank my loved ones in Spirit for being with me today.
Thank you for helping me to receive my desire and for guiding
my path, now and throughout my life. I ask my loving family
in spirit to help me as I open to receiving my greatest
and highest good. And so it is.

Help Is on the Way

Whether you choose to ask your cosmic helpers for assistance or not is really up to you. You will be able to manifest if you do or do not contact them. They are working for you behind the scenes as we speak. The purpose of making a concerted effort to consciously know them is to make your attempt stronger and more powerful by using heavenly fuel to light the engine of your desire. It stands to reason that the more power we can generate, the faster and more fulfilling the results. It is also important to acknowledge them and their contributions to our lives.

Since the process of getting everything you ever wanted is not an exact science, you may choose to work with one energy more often than another. You may prefer to work with your angels daily and your guides weekly, seeking the help of your loved ones less frequently. This is an individual decision. The glory of it all is that we have the choice.

In the next chapter, we will focus on adding more energy to our process, using the powers that exist, right now, in our conscious and subconscious minds.

CHAPTER 8

Programming Your Success

*W*e humans have the capability to channel and focus extraordinary amounts of mental energy. This ability has been with us from birth, locked within our own minds. We can learn to develop the psychic skills that enable us to get everything we want by delving into the core of our being: our subconscious mind.

Affording us more ammunition to further our goals, we can learn how psychic ability, dreams, and autohypnosis can help us get what we want. Our psychic talents, gifts to us from the Universe at birth, can be developed and honed so that we begin to rely on them as second nature. They are more reliable than logic.

Children of a technological society, we Westerners rely heavily on our rational mind to make decisions. Unfortunately, the logical mind cannot always compute the illogical elements of our nature, such as our emotions and feelings. These are not rational at all, yet many of us depend on them to make life choices. I am suggesting that we become open to reliance upon our intuitive, psychic mind rather than our logical or emotional aspects. When we do, our choices become more accurate because we are following the prompting of our inner or God self, and God is always right.

Every minute of our lives, our subconscious mind is at work in our daily activities and even when we sleep. Dreams hold treasures of psychic information, clues to solutions to our problems, and energy usable for manifesting. It's hard to believe that you can be working on drawing what you want into your life while you are catching some Zs, but it's true.

The ultimate use of our subconscious mind occurs when we direct our attention to it by deliberately programming it. When we program our minds, we put forth a plan of action to accomplish a specific end. We use a sequence of instructions, a schedule to be followed, that sets our mind in motion toward our goal, and focuses it on success.

Our first task is understanding the level of our psychic ability to date. Knowing how much psychic common sense we already possess helps us recognize hidden psychic messages in our everyday lives.

You Must Be Psychic!

Most of the time we ignore the psychic messages that are continually bombarding our consciousness because we are not trained to perceive them. When the phone rings, do you sometimes know who is on the other end, even before you answer it? If you are a parent, do you just know when your kids are in trouble? Can you finish someone else's sentences? Are you often right when you give a friend advice? If you answered "yes" to any of these questions, well, then, you *must* be psychic!

Psychic messages are not always the predictive kind. They are disguised in our day-to-day thoughts. The reason we don't think of these messages as particularly psychic is because we expect too much. The hocus-pocus media hype that accompanies psychic hotlines tends to confuse the average person into believing that this ability is reserved for a select few. The prediction aspect is emphasized, rather than the perceptive one.

There is much more to being psychic than foretelling the future. Psychic ability includes the sensitivity to the here and now—awareness, on a much keener level, of what is happening immediately around you. As you develop this particular ability, you get in flow with the energy of the Universe. Being in flow means you easily attract opportunities to get what you want and, more importantly, you recognize when your intention is manifesting. You are able to pick up hints from the Universe that what you have asked for is actually on its way into your life. Seeing the initial phases of your request coming into your reality is comforting, and helps you remain patient while waiting for the final outcome. In chapter 9, I'll talk more about picking up on these intuitive messages in every facet of our lives.

Our psychic ability can be nurtured and stretched just like our physical muscles. The more you work at developing this talent, the stronger it becomes. Don't expect dramatic results the first few times you try your hand at honing your psychic mind. Like everything else, it takes practice, practice, and more practice. I can assure you that if you devote some time to it, you will be rewarded with patience, uncanny insight, and extraordinary intuition.

Discover the Psychic Within

Here are some exercises that will teach you to harness and develop your inner knowing. The more you practice them, the better you'll get at picking up vibrations and messages. Developing your psychic ability is a slow process, so don't expect amazing results overnight. Work with these exercises as often as you can, and you will begin to see the results in your everyday life. You will begin to feel calmer, less nervous about difficulties when they arise, and you will be able to instinctively know what to do in stressful situations. Over time, you will become more sensitive to the needs of others and be capable of giving sound advice from a stable perspective.

As you get more comfortable with attuning to this part of your psyche, you will notice others around you responding to you more favorably. You'll have fewer confrontations and disappointments. People cannot help but see a more peaceful difference in you, and they will respond in kind.

The benefits of developing your psychic mind are many. You will notice an expansion of your awareness of the world around you. The sky will look bluer and the clouds whiter than ever before. You will be in awe at the beauty of a flower, and you'll begin to see life with wonder. The most joyful byproduct of this development will be a recognition of your spiritual self, to know and experience more about your mind and soul. But the greatest gift you can give yourself in studying the intricacies of your mind is to enlarge your self-concept to include experiences that help you feel more alive, more in touch with others, and more a part of life. In other words, you will like and feel better about yourself!

Here are the exercises. It is always wise to begin this kind of exploration of the mind with a meditation. Meditation grounds you, calms you down, and clears the conscious mind of conflicting thoughts so it becomes receptive to messages from its psychic counterpart, the subconscious. I have included a meditation that you should use each time you begin this work. You may record it on an audiotape and use it as a guided meditation or commit it to memory. You may also use soft meditation music, if you like.

Exercise 19: Grounding Meditation

1. Close your eyes and take three deep breaths. Allow a wave of relaxation to move slowly through your body, starting at your head and slowly moving down, relaxing your mind, your neck, your shoulders, and slowly moving down your arms into your thighs and down through your legs. Feel this comforting wave of relaxation move into your feet and totally relax your body.

2. When you are totally relaxed, you feel and see a gentle cloud of white light and protection surrounding your body. You are safe.

3. Now, see in your mind's eye a beautiful silver cord projecting from the base of your spine, spiraling slowly down through your chair into the floor of the room and down into the ground. This beautiful silver spiraling cord moves deep into the core of the Earth and becomes one with it, branching out into beautiful silver roots, taking hold and grounding you to the Earth. Enjoy this oneness with the Earth for a moment.

4. Still relaxing, you feel peace and harmony with yourself and all of creation. It is as if time and space were suspended. You are one with the Universe.

5. Now, say the word "clear" to yourself, and open your mind to receive any psychic vibrations, messages, and information.

6. Relax for a moment, at peace.

7. Remaining in a clear and peacefully calm state, take a deep breath and, as you exhale slowly and deliberately, return to full consciousness and open your eyes.

You are now ready to begin the exercises.

Exercise 20: Feeling Your Energy

In this first exercise you will actually feel the energy that you project from your body. It is your psychic energy in physical form.

1. Sit comfortably, both feet on the ground. Raise your arms in front of you, palms facing each other, about two feet apart. Do not extend your arms straight out in front of you. Keep them close to your body, in a relaxed position, as though you were holding a very large beach ball between your hands.

2. Clear your mind, and gradually move your palms inward toward each other. As you do this, be aware of what you are feeling in your hands. You should begin to feel a slight magnetic pull as your hands slowly get closer together. Keep moving them inward, gently, until you feel the pull. If you do this too quickly, you won't feel it.

3. When you feel the slight tugging, begin to manipulate the energy ever so slightly. It will feel like a small, invisible ball between your hands. Pay attention to how it feels.

4. Repeat this exercise until you can feel the energy when your hands are very far apart.

As you become more sensitive to your own energy, you increase your sensitivity to the energy of others and the environment around you. You will perceive when other people are entering a room even when your back is to the door. When you enter a space that is positive or negative, you will feel it in your body, possibly as a change in temperature or as chills. This is a very important psychic skill to develop. It will get you out of uncomfortable or even dangerous situations. Trust your energy. It doesn't lie.

Psychometry

Psychometry is an ancient psychic skill where we attempt to connect with the energy of an inanimate object. It is a way we can pick up messages and vibrations from the object by holding it in our hands or placing our hands upon it. Remember, everything has energy and that energy stores information. Objects hold onto their own energy but they also pick up and absorb energy from the people and environment around them, just as we do. Have you ever held a coveted, well-loved object of your own and immediately felt better, happier, calmer? That's why children cling to their favorite teddy bear even after the fur has rubbed off and the eyes have fallen out. The treasured toy holds energy that is loving and comfortable. It holds the energy of the child himself, his love and affection for the piece. All things respond to love, even the ones we think are incapable of it. Energy is alive, even in inanimate objects, so keep that in mind and treat all your possessions with respect.

We're going to use this talent of psychometry in the next two exercises. They will develop your sensitivity to even greater levels and you'll be amazed at the results. You will need a friend to help you with them. Choose a friend who is sympathetic to what you're doing, and who'd like to experiment along with you.

Exercise 21: Psychometry—We've Got the Whole World in Our Hands!

For this first exercise, ask a friend to exchange a beloved object with you—one small enough to be held in the palms of both hands, such as a small statue or knickknack. We will attempt to perceive a history from the object. We'll ask it questions in our mind, trying to find out more about the energy stored within it. It is very important that you have never seen the object before and know nothing about it. But your friend must know everything about it so that he can confirm your perceptions. That is the whole point of this exercise. You will be able to determine how accurate your perceptions are through your friend. You can do this exercise alone, if you wish. Just get the object from your friend ahead of time and, instead of discussing the psychic vibrations you received in person, simply write them down. You can always discuss the findings over the phone or at a later date.

In receiving these messages, be prepared to accept the first thought that comes into your mind. It is usually the correct psychic vibration. Don't censor anything, and don't expect to hear words alone. Many people hear nothing but see pictures, colors, or just have a feeling that they know what the object is trying to convey. Just allow yourself to get a sense of it, and don't try too hard. You will get better with practice.

After doing the meditation relax, clear your mind, and hold the object with both hands. (Note that it is unnecessary to repeat the grounding meditation each time you do an exercise, if you are doing them all at one sitting.)

Close your eyes and allow information to come to you by focusing on the following questions, one at a time. Relax and be still after asking each question, and wait for some perception to come to you. Don't move on to the next question until you receive an answer, or until you instinctively feel you should. The object may not give you a response to all of the questions exactly. It might send its very own message instead. Share your perceptions with your friend after each question and see how accurate you are.

How old is this object?

Who gave it to your friend?

Why is it important to your friend?

What message does the object want to relay to you?

You should only spend about fifteen minutes on this exercise. I have had students so determined to get all the answers that they drive themselves into exhaustion. It's only an exercise. Take your time with your development, and you will eventually master it.

Exercise 22: Psychometry with Photographs

We are going to take the psychometry exercise a step further, doing much the same thing but using photographs. In my classes, this exercise always engenders oohs and ahs as students surprise themselves with their own ability.

This time, ask your friend to give you a photograph with people in it, or a special place, that he knows well but you have never met or seen. *Don't look at the picture!* Have your friend give it to you facing the photo to your palm, then close your other hand over it, like a sandwich. Or, better yet, put the photo in an envelope so you won't have the urge to peek. Hold it the same way, between the hands, one over the other. We will go through the same process as before, sharing your perceptions with your friend after each question.

Who or what is in the picture?

What is the gender, age, and appearance of the people?

Why is this place or these people important to your friend?

What message does the photo want to relay to you?

Again, spend only about fifteen minutes on this one, too. Give yourself time to develop this skill. It takes a little longer than the others, but you will discover a fascinating part of your mind, if you choose to explore it.

I hope you have enjoyed these exercises. If you are faithful and do them often, you will be in touch with your inner awareness and guidance. Developing your psychic ability through these various active techniques will open your channel to receive everything you want in life. It will teach you to focus your energy on your desires. This focus will act as a magnet, drawing them to you. Keener perceptions of the world and others around you will enable you to recognize the subtle changes that are happening in your life as your desires form and enter into physical reality.

Follow Your Dreams

Even while you sleep, you can create your future and send the message of your desires out to the Universe. We can successfully program our minds to receive insights concerning our intention and how to do our half in bringing it into reality. We can suggest to our subconscious mind that it supply us with this information using the archetypes or symbols in our dreams.

In manifesting, it is useful to establish sleep patterns to clear the mind. We can remove blocks to getting what we want and focus the message of our intention during our slumber. The majority of this conditioning will take place in the twilight time, just before we fall asleep. It is here that our minds are between the waking beta state and the dreaming alpha state. In this gap of deep relaxation, our minds are most susceptible to suggestions. This programming is very safe and cannot harm us in any way. The worst case is that it won't work at all, nothing more. I have taught this technique to my students and they have had great success with it. This mind programming is a form of auto- or self-hypnosis, and it is an easy and very effective tool.

Getting your dreams to work for you is simple. It does not require the extensive exercises that developing your psychic ability does, though it takes more time. You will need to commit to trying this technique over several weeks or until it works for you. The affirmations we will use are designed to build upon each other. It need not take as long. Everyone responds differently. Some people are successful the first time they attempt it, others take longer. Try each affirmation for a week. Do it every night for at least seven days, with no gaps in between. If it still doesn't work, take a break and try it again next month. If you get results immediately, then move to the next affirmation. Have patience if you are a slow mover. Like everything else, it takes time and repetition.

Exercise 23: Dream Programming, Week 1

1. When retiring for the evening, make sure you are as comfortable as possible.

2. As you recline, relax, and begin to calm down, say the following words to yourself until you fall asleep:

> *Tonight my dreams will focus and send the essence*
> *of my intention, (fill in your particular desire),*
> *to the Universe.*

That is all there is to it. This first week, our programming consists of reinforcing the message. You may notice that you are beginning to dream about your desire. That is excellent. It is the result we are going for, and means your subconscious is beginning to respond and filter the energy to your conscious mind. Not long after that, you will see it in physical form.

Exercise 24: Dream Programming, Week 2

Here is the second phase of our technique, where we remove any possible obstacles from our subconscious mind that might stand in the way of getting what we want:

1. When retiring for the evening, make sure you are as comfortable as possible.

2. As you recline, relax, and begin to calm down, say the following words to yourself until you fall asleep:

> *Tonight, in my dreams, I remove all blocks to*
> *receiving the essence of my intention,*
> *(fill in your particular desire here).*

Exercise 25: Dream Programming, Week 3

1. In this final phase, we ask for information to assist us in drawing what we want into our life:

Tonight, in my dreams, I receive help and guidance
to draw the essence of my intention,
(fill in your particular desire),
into my life.

This last programming affirmation opens the door to our subconscious to tell us directly what we can do to further our success.

General Notes About Dream Programming

Keep in mind that the responses you get when programming your dreams can come in allegorical or archetypal form. They may not be literal responses. Our dreams are seldom literal, and can often confuse us. The first two phases of this technique do not require dream interpretation at all. They simply send your intention via a focused message through your subconscious and then remove blocks to receiving it. The last phase asks our higher mind for information, requiring it to answer in the only way it knows: by creating mental pictures, or dreams.

Dreams require more work for us. We must understand what our own individual symbols are and learn to interpret them. This takes time and effort. You will still successfully use the power of the subconscious during sleep if you only do the first two phases. But if you are the anxious type and need answers, it would be a good idea to develop this third ability. Some of us are good at interpreting the symbols in our dreams, and will know immediately what they are trying to say. If you are not one of those lucky folks, my suggestion is to take a class in dream interpretation or try it on a small scale with the

exercises that follow. Don't try too hard or you could stop your flow of manifesting with frustration. Simply skip this third phase, and read on to chapter 9.
In it I'll give you exercises you can do to get the same answers from your subconscious while you're awake!

Exercise 26: Dream Work

Do these dream interpretation exercises when you have time, if you're interested in exploring this ability. You'll need to record your dreams in a journal
immediately upon awakening, lest you forget them. Keep it handy, near your
bed. Write your dreams down before you get out of bed in the morning, while
you're still in alpha state. After that, distractions could wreak havoc on your
memory.

> On this page, or in your journal, reflect on your dreams and write
> down any symbols that seem to recur in them, both pleasant and
> frightening. Think about your dreams in general, and see if you can
> spot your individual symbols. Record them here.

Now, write down any recurring dreams you may be having or might have had in the past. Are the symbols you previously recorded part of these dreams? Are there any new symbols you might have missed?

_____

_____

_____

_____

_____

_____

_____

_____

_____

Record the most recent dream you can remember. Analyze it by comparing it to the above symbols and/or recurring dreams. Are there similarities? Can you begin to see your dream patterns?

_____

_____

_____

_____

_____

_____

_____

_____

_____

After answering the above questions, begin your week-long dream analysis. Record all your dreams for a week in your journal. Then compare them to what is happening in your life right now. Even though they are extreme, can you see how the events in your dream may stand for something else that is currently going on in your life? Could one symbol really stand for something else? For instance, if you dream you are running away from someone whose intent is to hurt you, might you be running from responsibility, a relationship, or a conflict now happening in your world? Try to make these applications.

In all fairness to the fine men and women who have dedicated their lives to dream interpretation, I apologize for this quickie course but it has worked for my students on a very basic level. If your interest is great, get some professional training. For our manifesting purposes, we have learned all we need.

Hypnotizing Yourself

Self-hypnosis is yet another tool that can help us get what we want. It is also called autohypnosis, in which an individual hypnotizes himself instead of being put into a trance (deep relaxation) by another person. Self-hypnosis is yet another art that must be mastered with patience and practice. In manifesting, we use self-hypnosis to calm and relax the mind and focus it on drawing the desired intention to us as we tap into the power of the subconscious. You may be sitting in a doctor's office, waiting to see him, and use the time to hypnotize yourself to work on manifesting your desire. The process does not take long and can be done anywhere, except in a moving car!

I am a certified hypnotherapist, and I find that doing self-hypnosis once a day revitalizes my energy and keeps me in touch with whatever it is I am trying to draw into my life at that point. Self-hypnosis is not for everyone but, after learning and trying the technique, you may judge for yourself.

It is important to understand that self-hypnosis will not work for you if you have any fears about it or are skeptical. This method requires that the subject (you) be willing. So, if you have any doubts, skip this tool.

Self-hypnosis consists of three main steps: relaxation, induction, and autosuggestion.

Relaxation

This first step requires the individual to totally relax. The environment must be comfortable and quiet. You should be totally alone. It is up to the individual to relax him- or herself and feel at peace, clearing the mind of all thoughts.

Induction

The induction is merely a deepening of the relaxation accompanied by a key word, which works as a suggestion to the mind that hypnosis is taking place. You would choose a word that represents relaxation to you, a sort of mantra, such as "peace," "serenity," "calm." It works as a trigger so that when you repeat it to yourself it deepens the relaxation.

Autosuggestion

This is the meat of the process. After you have completed the first two steps and are in the state of hypnosis, you must make suggestions to yourself. For our purposes, the suggestions in the form of a sentence are similar to the affirmations we have been using. You simply state the chosen affirmations to yourself until you feel they have been absorbed by your subconscious mind. This is totally subjective. You will instinctively know when you have repeated the suggestions enough.

The following is the self-hypnosis technique. Remember to be alone in a quiet environment, and don't be afraid. The worst that can happen is that it just doesn't work. You can record the relaxation, induction, and autosuggestion techniques on audiotape, and play it during the entire session. Make sure your voice is soothing.

Exercise 27: The Self-Hypnosis Technique

Find a quiet place. Sit up in a chair, feet flat on the floor, and relax. You may play ocean or nature tapes, if you like.

Begin the relaxation by closing your eyes, taking three deep breaths, and telling yourself the following *slowly* and *soothingly*:

I am now relaxing. I am calm and at peace. I feel a wave of relaxation moving from the top of my head to the tip of my toes. I focus on the crown of my head and feel the relaxation moving down my face, relaxing all my facial muscles.

The relaxation moves down around the back of my head, relaxing my neck and shoulders. My head, neck, and shoulders are totally relaxed. The relaxation now moves down my arms, all the way to my fingertips. My arms are now totally relaxed. And the relaxation moves down from my shoulders over my torso, relaxing my upper and lower back, moving down around my waist and hips, relaxing them. My torso, back, and hips are totally relaxed. The relaxation now moves down over my thighs, my knees, and over the calves of my legs.

My thighs, knees, and legs are now totally relaxed. The wave of relaxation continues to move down over the tops of my feet and out to my toes, and under the soles of my feet. My feet are totally relaxed. My entire body is totally relaxed. I am now totally relaxed and at peace.

Now it is time to add the words of induction to deepen the state. Choose a key word that represents relaxation to you, such as "peace," "serenity," or "calm," and repeat it to yourself at least five or six times or until you sense you are deeper into a relaxing, trancelike state.

Finally, add your autosuggestion affirmation, repeating it until you feel it has been absorbed by your subconscious. Repeat it a minimum of five to six times. You may use the following affirmation, or write your own:

> *I draw (fill in your desire) to me now.*
> *_____ comes to me now easily, safely,*
> *and in a loving way. I am a magnet for _____.*
> *It is now a part of my life and reality.*
> *It comes to me now.*

To awaken from self-hypnosis, you simply need to suggest to yourself just that. When your autosuggestion has been absorbed, say the following to return to full consciousness:

> *On the count of three, I will be wide awake and return to full*
> *consciousness, relaxed, refreshed, and full of energy—*
> *one, two, three!*

Remember to awaken from your hypnotic state deliberately. If you forget this part and simply open your eyes, you'll be groggy for awhile. It is important to return to full waking consciousness. The final suggestion brings you back full of get-up-and-go!

Theory and Practice

As you have learned in this chapter, programming yourself to draw whatever you want into your life is useful, fun, peaceful, and successful. Discovering your level of psychic ability and then developing it enables you to not only direct your world but to perceive the changes happening in it. Analyzing your dreams gives you greater insight into your own subconscious mind as well as gives you another way of reinforcing and refocusing your energy to send your intention out to the Universe. Finally, self-hypnosis enables you to implant your desire deeper into the realm of the subconscious, thereby influencing the strongest element of your mind.

In the chapter to follow, we will turn within and give more serious thought to our innermost prompting—our intuition.

CHAPTER 9

Listening to Your Intuition

*H*ave you ever done something you just knew or felt you shouldn't do? Others might have urged you to do it, but after the situation is over, you regretted it. You found yourself saying, "Something was telling me not to do that, and I did it anyway." That "something" was your intuition, that little gnawing voice inside your head. It can be relentlessly persistent as it endeavors to save us from ourselves, no matter how hard we try to ignore it. Intuition is another inner ability all humans possess. Learning to listen to its voice within us, and act upon its strong advice, will enable us to create the life we want and deserve.

Our intuition influences every facet of our lives. It is part of our psychic common sense. In order to make our intuitive mind work for us and help us get everything we want, we must learn to recognize how it shows up in our lives each day. We can monitor our manifesting by paying attention to early signposts indicating we are on the right track. Your intuition will help you to become aware that you are in the process of manifesting your desires. It will awaken your perception of the world around you so you will clearly recognize that you are actually receiving what you have asked for.

Your intuition will enable you to identify that your intention is being demonstrated in your life through synchronistic events. It is so easy for us to miss these often subtle, outward indications and pawn them off as coincidences. We don't believe these fortuitous circumstances to be the Universe in action, working to assist us in drawing our desires into our lives. There are no coincidences. The Universe is not random. It is planned and systematic. We get what we want, situations arise, and people come into our lives, responding to the plan of energy we set forth.

Let us say you are trying to manifest a new home. There are many steps in that process that need to come together so you can purchase it. You must locate a real estate agent, go house-hunting, find a mortgage lender, be approved for that mortgage, retain an attorney to help you close the deal, etc., etc., etc. Many of us don't realize that the Universe starts working when we do, the minute we put forth our energy in a focused direction. In other words, when we finally decide we want to purchase a house, the Cosmic Dynamo kicks into action. It functions along with us, within the framework of the world we live in. The Universe doesn't necessarily bypass the steps but rather allows opportunities to present themselves and simplifies what could be complicated endeavors. So, you find a real estate agent, love the first house you look at, are immediately approved for a mortgage, and your brother-in-law is an attorney! Everything you need seems to mysteriously be there, when and where you need it. This is not coincidence, it is synchronicity. Who engineers synchronicity? The Universe.

Your intuition will help you to relax and see that things are happening in your favor. It will keep you on track by helping you to make the correct choices within the manifesting process to carry it to fruition. When buying your house, you can depend upon your intuition to guide you to the *right* real estate agent, the *right* home, the *right* bank, and even the *right* lawyer. The *right* people, things, or situations are the ones that are in your highest and greatest good. Your inner prompting will let you know if they are not.

Listening to your intuition to achieve your heart's desires is an interesting and very successful practice. I find that I will no longer make an important decision in my life without consulting the Wise One within. Incidentally, it is always correct because its source is Spirit, or God.

Creative Feeling

You've heard of creative thinking. Your intuition is your creative *feeling*. It is that inner sense of knowing that is beyond all logic. The word itself means inner teaching, and comes from the Latin *intueri*, which means looking or knowing from within. Your intuition is not rational, logical, or based on any experience. It is basically inborn, a part of your mind.

Your intuitive ability is different from your psychic ability. It draws mainly from your subconscious mind to help you make life decisions and solve problems. Psychic ability can draw from lots of sources and is not limited to your subconscious. Psychics can receive information from contact with outside energies such as angels, spirit guides, or those loved ones who have passed away. The important distinction is that your intuition is very personal, and is focused on you. The information comes from you, for you. Psychic ability is impersonal in that the information comes *through* you, possibly from an outside source, and is not necessarily *for* you. The messages may be given to you but can be meant to help someone else.

Intuitive messages are less obvious than psychic messages. We need to interpret our intuitive messages. Psychic messages can come in ways that need no interpretation, such as in visions, words, and sentences. Because they are so subjective, intuitive impressions require us to pay close attention to our responses—mentally, emotionally, and physically.

When an intuitive message from your subconscious filters through to your conscious mental and emotional sensors, you can recognize it because it is usually a sudden, spontaneous thought or an immediate insight, like a light bulb going on in your head. It is the kind of thought that feels as though a switch has been flipped from "off" to "on" in your mind, and you know exactly what to do about a particular situation. It is not snap decision-making, because accompanied by this sudden knowledge is a feeling that it is right. You are confident, and follow the thought willingly.

For example, you might be confused about where to go on vacation. You and your sweetie are looking at travel brochures. A myriad of possibilities is available to you. You'd love to go to Aspen skiing but, as you gaze at the happy faces in the pictures slaloming down the gorgeous mountains, you nix the idea, thinking that you'd love to go there but *something* is telling you not to. It just doesn't seem right. Then, you see a brochure of the Bahamas. "That's it!" you say. Yes, you *feel* it is the *perfect* place to go, and (surprise, surprise) it's more affordable than Aspen (another nudge from the Universe). Your intuition is kicking in.

Added to our mental and emotional responses is a physical one. Looking at your travel brochures of the Bahamas, you not only know and feel it's the right destination, your body literally responds with physical signs. Your heart starts to race, your body gets warm and excited, and the adrenaline pumps. You're ready to leap off the couch to go purchase the airline tickets. This reaction is the ultimate response to the situation. Your body is also intuitively telling you, through its positive reaction, that your decision is the correct one.

Let's look at another response. Viewing the pictures of Aspen leaves you with an uneasy feeling (emotional), and you have your doubts (mental). Your body is signaling discomfort as you shift in your seat, sense a headache coming on, and there is a funny feeling in your gut. Your gut goes beyond your stomach, clear through to the core of your being. This part of you is definitely saying no, too.

Our intuition speaks to us on all levels of our being. We know if we like a person or not by our gut response to them. All of us have had this experience at one time or another. Either we click with someone, or we can't stand them. These extreme situations indicate our intuition is in full gear. If we listen to it, we'll be right. How many times have you ignored someone's faults within a relationship, and years later find yourself saying, "I just knew he wasn't right for me the day I met him!" Pay more attention to your intuitive responses to other people and you will never have a bad date, shifty lawyer, obnoxious doctor, or dishonest friend again.

Your environment also communicates with your intuitive self. Pay attention to the feeling or energy in the air. Is it comfortable or not? Cues will be obvious when you develop this skill. Your body will usually respond first in these situations. You might actually feel a temperature change, a tingling in your hands or fingers, or difficulty breathing. Then, your mind and emotions respond with an uncomfortable or uneasy feeling. I have been known to walk right in and out of a store because I sensed that the energy in the place was negative. My mind-body intuitively responds and I feel all the uncomfortable emotions, as well as a shortness of breath. Of course, your body will tell you to get out of there, in its own way. If it does, beat it! Spirit is giving you a direct signal that you're in the wrong place at the wrong time.

Your intuition can assist you in making choices that are right and perfect for you, and in your greatest good. You must simply practice focusing your attention on your reactions to people, places, situations, and things. If this skill is new to you, the following exercises can help you recognize your intuitive responses.

Exercise 28: Getting to Know You

The way we make decisions can tell us a great deal about how intuitive we are. Ask yourself the following questions and record your answers in the space below or in your journal.

1. How do you make decisions? What is your personal process? Do you think for a long time, mull over all the possibilities forever, come to a conclusion quickly, etc.?

_____

_____

_____

_____

_____

_____

_____

_____

2. Do you make quick or snap decisions? How often? What happens when you do? Are you right? Do you regret it or not? Does it usually work for you or not?

_____

_____

_____

_____

_____

_____

_____

_____

3. Do you think you make incorrect decisions most of the time, some of the time, or seldom? What makes you think so?

_____

_____

_____

_____

_____

_____

_____

_____

_____

_____

4. Do you like making decisions, or do you hate it? Why or why not?

_____

_____

_____

_____

_____

_____

_____

_____

_____

These are just a few simple questions that can tell you plenty. Read over your answers. There are no right or wrong responses. This exercise is one of self-evaluation and assessment. Here are the general observation guidelines for each question. Determine what applies to you, and go forward from there.

Question 1

Your response to this question should give you a pretty good idea of yourself as a decision maker. Did you ever realize how long it takes you to make a decision, or how quickly you do? It should not take forever, nor should you make any determination in haste. Either case indicates that you are not allowing your intuitive mind to assist you. If you take too long, you are relying too heavily on your logical mind and you can go around in circles a million times before you get on track. If you decide too quickly, you ignore your intuitive perceptions because you are either nervous, angry, or just plain impatient. You are not giving yourself the opportunity to receive guidance. It will take you much longer to get what you want.

Question 2

Most of the time, snap decisions do not work in your favor. You are neither relying on your logical mind nor your intuitive mind. You don't really stand a good chance at making an accurate decision if you only base it on emotion, which is, technically, what determines a snap decision. For the moment, you feel motivated to get the decision over with, but you set yourself up for a fall because it is not based on anything sound. When you decide, you feel good (at least temporarily) but your euphoria soon wanes when you realize you didn't take enough time and probably could have made a better choice. If you had listened to your intuition, you would have made the right decision the first time. We usually have to go back and repair damage caused by snap decisions. Unfortunately, we do not always have that opportunity. Your snap decision may work out for you at times, usually when the decision is trivial. But, it will not work often, if at all, when the choice is an important or life-changing one. Leave those to your higher mind.

Question 3

If you think you can't make a decision or make the wrong ones often, either your self-esteem is at an all-time low or you are having trouble interpreting your own logical thoughts. This could indicate a psychological problem. Examine your reasons why you are having trouble. Are you blaming others or the situation? Most of us struggle with major decisions. We get bombarded with doubts and can often make the wrong choices. All of us have been in that boat from time to time. But if you are always tormented by having to make a decision, you need to get clinical help to clear your logical mind so that you can give your intuitive mind an open channel. Confusion gets in the way of manifesting. You will do well to develop some trust in yourself. Even the great thinkers of history made a few awful choices. The point is, they got back on track, possibly following an inner prompting that let them know they would be okay if they just calmed down, and reevaluated the circumstances with an eye toward their inner wisdom. Do you know how many bummers Thomas Edison designed before he got the light bulb right? Plenty.

Question 4

Do we really like making decisions? Life seems to be one momentous choice after another. Decision-making is both the most trying and ultimately creative part of life. If you are a person who likes making decisions, you will get everything you ever wanted faster than anyone you know. If you hate doing it, you probably should stop reading now because getting what you want requires enthusiasm for life and the active participation in its every aspect. If you sometimes enjoy making decisions, and sometimes not, join the club. Most of us fall into this area. It's called being human, but it is also known as being balanced. For the difficult times, rely on your intuition to help you decide, and your accurate decisions will get easier and easier to make.

For Fun and Profit

The following two exercises are designed to develop your intuition. In the above exercise, you analyzed your willingness and accuracy in making choices. Now, you will ask your intuitive mind to tell you what you need to know. Yes, it is possible to get direct answers from your intuition, but you must first know how intuitive you already are.

My students enjoy this self-discovery process and have fun doing this next exercise. It will teach you to accept your first impressions without censoring them with logic. First responses are usually our intuitive ones. I created this exercise when I was invited to lecture in a local grade school. I worked with students in science classes from the first to the fifth grades. The children had lots of fun discovering their intuitive ability. You can use this exercise with your own children, if you like, but master it yourself first. Recently, I used it at my ministerial convention in which hundreds of my peers, all adults, tried it. Most of these folks thought they were already intuitive. Needless to say, there were many surprises. By the way, the kids scored higher than the adults. Logic and age has a way of complicating our lives.

Exercise 29: Develop Your Intuition

Enlist the assistance of a compassionate friend to perform this exercise. You will need an envelope, any small business-size will do, but make sure you can't see through it. You will also need two sheets of colored paper, in two different colors.

1. Cut two small rectangles, about 2 by 3 inches in size, from each of the two different colored papers. You will have a total of four rectangles, two of each color.

2. Now, take two of the rectangles, one of each color, and leave the room. While you are out of the room, your friend should choose one of the two remaining colored rectangles and place it in the envelope. The other colored rectangle should be hidden somewhere out of sight.

3. Reenter the room when your friend is finished. Sit down in a comfort-able chair, relax, close your eyes, and take three deep breaths, clearing your mind. Hold both rectangles in your hands. Your intuition is going to tell you the color of the rectangle inside the envelope.

4. Keep your mind calm and clear, and the moment you have a vision, sense, feeling, or a knowing of one of those two colors, hold up that color paper for your friend to see.

5. Determine your results.

If at first you succeed, good for you. You are listening to your intuition. To make sure it wasn't a lucky guess, try it at least four or five more times. It you are correct every time, or at least three out of four times, pat yourself on the back and move on to the next exercise. Not so good? Then keep at it until you are right at least three out of four times. This will flex your intuitive muscle and train you to accept your first accurate impressions.

Exercise 30: Choose the High Road

Amazingly, it is possible to get yes or no answers from your intuitive mind. My students (and peers) have found this exercise most helpful when they are too emotional to recognize and interpret the signals from their higher mind. This tool involves visualization, a skill that you have mastered well by now. You will not need anything but your mind and your willingness to try.

1. Sit down in a comfortable chair. Relax, close your eyes, and take three deep breaths, clearing your mind.

2. Keep your mind calm and clear. You are going to allow your subcon-scious to form a picture of two roads in your mind, one at a time. First, tell your intuitive self to show you what your "yes" road looks like. Permit the picture to form, and don't censor it. Help it along with your imagination.

(My road has light-colored pavement, and is lined with beautiful trees, plants, and flowers. It winds happily and looks inviting.)

3. Next, tell your intuitive self to show you what your "no" road looks like. Permit the picture to form, and don't censor it. Help it along with your imagination.

    (Mine has black pavement, and appears to be crossing a desert. There are no trees or greenery evident. It feels ominous to me. I'm not taking that one!)

4. Now that you have a visualization of each road, take another deep breath and clear your mind.

5. Begin to form a question in your mind that needs an immediate "yes" or "no" answer.

6. Silently focus on the question for a moment, then let it go and wait for the picture of one of your roads to appear in your mind. You've got your answer.

Your intuition has given you the best response. Now you must trust it. Use this tool whenever you need it, but try not to depend on it alone. Allow your other intuitive perceptions—the mental, emotional, and physical ones I described earlier—to work for you as well.

Opening to Your Intuition

Messages from your intuitive self can also come through in your meditations. I use a light trance state to induce the above exercises through breathing, but if you program your intuition in meditation, you can tell it to become more pronounced and to send clearer messages to you when you are in beta state, your everyday level of awareness.

We can receive clear, unmistakable information when we are calm and unemotional, anytime and anywhere. Here is a thumbnail guide to follow to enable your intuition to flow when you are going about your daily life. When you need to make a decision, or for immediate assistance in a particular situation, call upon your higher wisdom by relaxing and doing the following:

1. **Breathe** (Three deep breaths are always effective.)

2. **Center** (Calm down and clear your mind.)

3. **Allow/Listen/Wait** (Allow your intuition to flow, don't think, just wait for an impression.)

4. **Interpret** (Let the mental, emotional, or physical impression affect you. Respond to it, and recognize it as positive or negative.)

5. **Relax** (Take time to think about it calmly.)

6. **Give Thanks/Act** (Thank the Universe for the information, and do what it tells you to do. Make your choice.)

This simple method will work for you when all else fails. Your intuition is always present and doesn't depend on any outside force. It is available to you whenever you need it. The intuitive part of your mind will respond to situations even when you do not call on it. It is there to keep you on track in making choices, protect and warn you about possible negativity, and help you to recognize when you are beginning to draw your desires into your life.

When you get accustomed to relying on your intuition, you will easily recognize the signs that it offers. What you must not do is block the flow of this guidance with doubt, confusion, fear, or logic.

Your intuition uses the illogical in a logical way. The impressions you receive on a mental, physical, or emotional level are not logical, yet they happen through a logical process. For instance, you might enter an unfamiliar store to do some shopping. Your body begins to react and you feel stifled and out of breath. Your emotions respond and you sense that you do not like it there. You want to leave, which you just might do, depending upon the severity of the discomfort. All of this occurs in logical sequence, masterminded by the part of your psyche that is acutely perceptive. This subconscious mind triggered the conscious responses. The quality of your life may depend upon whether you are aware of its influence or not, and whether you heed its guidance or choose not to do so. Seems logical to me!

In my intuition classes, I leave my students with the following final thoughts about developing this psychic common sense skill. As you work on perfecting your awareness of your intuitive mind, keep these ideas in mind.

- Accept any and all intuitive messages.

- Don't make judgments about what you are seeing, feeling, or thinking. Let it flow.

- Trust your first impressions or the initial intuitive response to the situation.

- Accept your less than dramatic or weaker responses, the ones that don't seem strong, because they are valid, too.

- Don't tell yourself, "It's just me making this all up." Have faith.

- Believe intuitive messages in whatever form you receive them—physically, mentally, or emotionally.

- Trust your intuitive responses whether they are spontaneous or you have asked for a reply.

- Don't complicate the process by thinking too much. The intuitive messages are usually simple.

- Call upon this skill often and know that it is working in your highest good.

Spiritual Intuition

The God within you has created this phenomena of intuition in order to urge us to pay attention to our spiritual self. Intuition defies logic and encourages us to depend more on our inner guidance. Our intuition is spiritual because its wisdom is not dependent on our mind or body. Its knowledge comes from our Creator, our Source, the Universe itself. We are more than just a mind and body, we are a spirit, more powerful than we could ever imagine. Listening to the call of your intuition opens your spiritual channels and allows your inner wisdom to guide your every decision, thought, and act. Drawing on this unlimited source, we humans can do great things. We can become anything we choose and have whatever we want. Your intuition is your silent partner in life, always working for you and waiting to help.

You can strengthen your intuitive power by using a simple affirmation. Say it before you begin to work on this skill, or while you are perfecting it. Say it when you are confused by your intuitive impressions and need clarity or confirmation that you are becoming more aware. In short, this affirmation will help to open your mind and heart to your inner guide.

> *My intuition is strong, clear, and accurate.*
> *I am open to all impressions that come to me*
> *through the working of my intuition,*
> *a sacred and vital part of my inner wisdom.*

Are you willing now to let your inner guide, the God within, lead your way to happiness? Your answer should undoubtedly be, "Yes!" In the chapter to follow, I'll give you my sure-fire plan for getting what you want. My six steps to manifesting and your strong inner power are all you need to create a life of joy, success, and happiness.

CHAPTER 10

Six Steps to the Stars

*C*ongratulations! You are now ready to create the life you want. In the previous chapters, I have given you the basics of manifesting your desires. Now it is time to put those words into action. Manifesting is much easier than it seems. Included in this chapter is my sure-fire method for drawing whatever you want into your life. These six steps synthesize the entire focus of this book and put the basic formula for manifesting into a simple to follow and easy to understand form, usable for quick reference. If you have read the previous chapters, and I hope you have, you will appreciate this condensed version when you set out to do your manifesting. The steps are also included as part of this book's cover, designed as a removable pocket guide so you can keep the steps handy, without having to refer back to the book.

Before we move forward, I need to restate that you must always use your psychic common sense to get everything you want. Accept full responsibility for what you've requested, regardless of the circumstances that might arise surrounding it. Remember, you need to be careful and absolutely sure of what you want, and the essence of it must be perfectly clear to you. Scattered thoughts produce scattered results. Be wise, and do not try to manipulate others to get what you want. That is a no-no. All your work must be done in the highest and greatest good of all those who are involved.

Be realistic. Unless you are willing to do all it takes, you will not manifest your intention. The Universe only does *half* of the work, and *you* do the rest. You must understand and accept that commitment. What you want will come to you when you realize that you must make the effort to attract it. "Yes, but isn't reading this book and following the steps an effort?" you ask. Well, it is, but it is minor compared to what you must be willing to do to fulfill your heart's desires.

The six steps of manifesting get the ball rolling, focus your energy, and send the message of what you want to the Universe. You are responsible for being consistent and recognizing through your synchronistic, everyday events that what you want is coming to you. Taking advantage of opportunities, doors that are flung open for you by the Universe, is your responsibility and constitutes half of the work. Become aware of helpful people who are placed in your path. This, too, is part of your obligation. Creating an environment for success, acting successful, thinking positively, persevering, and staying enthusiastic are vital to your accomplishment.

It is not enough to simply read this book, perform the steps, and then just wait. If you do that, you'll be waiting forever. Action is the key. Don't drop the ball, keep moving. If you set a realistic goal, it will be yours. You are in partnership with the Universe, and you've got to pull your weight.

I think you understand the seriousness of what you need to do. So what follows are the six steps to the stars! Keep the image of reaching for the stars in mind. Go for the gusto! Don't hold back because you think you don't deserve something. The Universe wants you to have what you want. If what you desire is to be at the top of the ladder, don't settle for the second rung because you believe, "That's for special people. Not for people like me." Reach for the stars and you will fly with angels!

The Six Steps: Your Keys to Success

Step One

Proclaim it!

By now, you understand that you must make a clear, decisive choice in order to draw what you want into your life. So many possibilities await. It is truly up to you to prioritize your needs and wants, and understand the difference between the two. If you are still having trouble with this, refer back to chapter 1. Take control, clear your mind, and set your sights on success.

Tap into your inner power, and let your intuition help you to understand the essence of your intention. Get to the root, the substance, of what you want. Don't settle for less. Focus on the underlying source of your desire. It may be love, prosperity, abundance, or perfect health, whatever. Recognize *exactly* what is at the heart of your request, then proclaim it to high heaven! Invest your energy into your decision by telling yourself, "This is what I want, and what will come into my life!" If you need help deciding and focusing on the essence of your desire, go back and take a look at chapter 4.

If you're still confused about what you want, here is an affirmation to help you out.

I have decided exactly what I want (or need) at this moment,
and I clearly recognize and accept the physical manifestation
of its essence into my life. And so it is!

Step Two

Affirm it!

This is the *Say It* part of your process. Do you remember this from chapter 4? If not, go back and take a look. It is crucial that you develop your intention as a written affirmation to add energy and substance to your manifesting. Take ample time to create your message. Words are very powerful. Choose them carefully, according to the method I have given you. This step is the crux of your manifesting ritual. Without a stated and declared intention, you cannot expect the Universe to understand you. Voicing your need precisely and deliberately sends an unmistakable message to the Universe that you know what you want and are determined to get it.

It is important to follow the affirmation form to the letter. Your statement must reflect positivity and convey a sense of determination and resolve. It must be powerful. The affirmation must be worded as though you already have what you are asking for. Again, this reflects certainty, and the Universe will surely support it.

Here is an affirmation to help you write your affirmation!

I put my intention into words easily. I state my wants
(or needs) clearly, positively, and confidently. My affirmation
tells the Universe exactly what I want. And so it is!

Step Three

Sanctify it!

You must now perform your private ritual within a sacred space. The ritual you create here sanctifies your intention and adds to its power, so it must be done in a very private, personal space, one that is yours and yours alone. This sacred space is crucial to your manifesting, so make sure you choose it wisely. Look for a place that will remain relatively undisturbed, whether you are there or not. If you cannot dedicate a particular area for your altar, than be creative. It is important that no one move or touch any of your personal ritual items. Someone else's energy will upset the balance you are trying to create.

Select your ritual items carefully and with an eye toward enhancing your intention. This step follows the affirmation step so that you may choose the tools you wish to work with based upon your intention, i.e., coins or dollar bills, if it's money you want to draw. Whatever items you decide upon will be fine. They are only enhancements, nothing more. Remember, your mind and thoughts draw what you want into your life, but it is enjoyable and comforting to use tangible expressions.

Above all, don't forget a candle. "Have candle, will travel," is my motto. A candle is portable, so you can do your work anywhere—in a hotel room, your office, or outdoors on a camping trip. That way, you can have your material focus point anytime you want it. By the way, don't forget matches!

If all you do is light a candle, use it to focus your mind and send your message to the Universe; you will have done enough.

Flip back to chapter 6 for any other questions concerning your sacred space and how to sanctify your ritual items by blessing and charging them.

Are you having trouble finding a space to do your manifesting, or worried about others disturbing it? This affirmation will help.

I already have the perfect, beautiful space in which to do
my spiritual work. The space remains safe and undisturbed
at all times. It is divinely protected. And so it is!

Step Four

Energize it!

In this step, you prepare your body, mind, and spirit to receive what you have requested. Don't even think of skipping this step! (Don't skip *any* of them for that matter!) But this one literally focuses every part of your being toward your goal by gathering your psychic and spiritual energy. Even though energizing may imply a forceful action, our energy must be contained to manifest. It must be harnessed to build strength. Focused energy can change matter, scattered energy has no effect. A quiet but extremely powerful energy reserve is what we're going for here. It is rather easy to accomplish.

To energize your intention, you have to breathe. Breathing calms you down, concentrates your energy, slows down your body processes, and makes it easy for you to enter a light alpha state of relaxation. It gets you ready for your meditation and visualization.

Before you begin your ritual, either sitting, standing, or kneeling in your sacred space, take three deep cleansing breaths. Inhale through the nose and exhale through the mouth. Closing your eyes is a good idea. The process is more peaceful that way, and you avoid any distractions.

When the breathing is complete, say a short prayer asking the Universe to put a circle of white light and protection around you and your sacred space, as I stated in the sample ritual in chapter 6.

Finally, pause a moment with your eyes closed, in silence. Allow your heart to slow its beating, and all thoughts to clear from your mind. Relax. When you feel you are strong and ready, begin the ritual.

Here is the white circle affirmation I use.

There is a circle of God's white light and protection all around me and this sacred space. Only positive, loving energies can enter this circle. Negativity may not enter here. And so it is!

Step Five

Invoke it!

It is time now to perform your ritual. In order for the Universe to perceive and act upon what you want, you have to send out a cosmic wake-up call. In other words, you have to invoke the powers of the Universe by sending your clear message through word and action. This invocation summons the power to your aid. Once you call upon it, nothing can stop it!

I have outlined the sample ritual for you in chapter 6. Copy that page and keep it near you when you first begin manifesting rituals. Eventually, you won't need it. I have found that sequence to be most effective but you will adjust it to meet your own needs as time goes on.

For now, stick with the sequence I gave you, so there is no chance you will leave out something crucial. Follow the process carefully.

Should you decide not to perform such an elaborate ritual, then simply find a quiet place. After gathering your energy, state your affirmation. Then do your visualization meditation. That will be enough.

There is an affirmation for everything, even for the concern that the ritual is appropriate and effective. Here is an affirmation you can use.

My sacred ritual is blessed and right for my needs.
It complements my intention perfectly and is totally effective.
And so it is!

Step Six

Give thanks for it!

Your ritual is not complete, nor is your message properly sent to the Universe, until you give thanks to the Source of your joy, the very Power that makes it all happen for you. That is our sixth and final step.

If you skip this step, you might as well forget about getting what you want. You obviously have not gotten the point of the whole thing! Your good comes to you from Spirit, if you demonstrate a grateful heart. I'll go into detail on this in chapter 12. For now, try to grasp this notion—the Universe supports those who show that they value the process of life. Those who receive the most in this lifetime are the ones who realize that giving *precedes* getting, not the other way around. When you give thanks first, you give God your heart, devotion, trust, and love. There are no greater gifts. For this selfless beneficence, you are richly rewarded. Get it?

Way back in chapter 6, I followed the visualization meditation with a prayer of thanks. I know that thanks is included in your affirmation, but I feel the need to repeat the expression of gratitude. It can't hurt, and always makes me feel good. The following prayer/affirmation is the one I use. Copy it or write your own. Just don't forget it!

I thank the Universe for this (state your intention again),
which is already mine. I receive it into my life now, and thank
you for sending it to me in a safe and loving way, in the highest
good of everyone concerned. For this, and for my life,
I give thanks. And so it is!

One More Time

If you are like me, you like to see the whole picture at a glance. The following list is for you. Here is your future at a glance!

Six Steps to the Stars

Step One: Proclaim it!

Decide what you want, and focus on its essence.

Step Two: Affirm it!

Write down your intention as an affirmation.

Step Three: Sanctify it!

Prepare your sacred space.

Step Four: Energize it!

Gather your psychic and spiritual energy.

Step Five: Invoke it!

Perform your ritual.

Step Six: Give thanks for it!

There you have it—my sure-fire steps to getting everything you ever wanted . . . but we're not done yet! It is time to pull out all the stops and draw on our hidden talent to enhance and strengthen our efforts. In the next chapter, we'll discover how our own individual creativity can give our manifesting one last blast of energy, and make certain that it will be successful!

PART THREE

Pulling Out All the Stops

CHAPTER 11

Using Everything You've Got

*I*f you are like most people I know, you don't consider yourself particularly creative. I prefer to think that you simply have not yet discovered the artist within. Those of us who have dabbled in the arts, having crafted ashtrays and pasta people at summer camp, know that creativity comes in many forms and takes on many guises. It may be surprising to you to know that the talent and artistic ability you possess can also assist you in getting everything you ever wanted. To draw what you want into your life, you have got to be prepared to use all the gifts, power, creativity, drive, skill, and knowledge that you've got. Every fiber of your being, heart, mind, and soul must work toward focusing upon your intention and sending a strong message of your heart's desire out to the Universe.

To be successful in your manifesting, you need to appreciate your artistic ability and resolve to use it. Your creativity is very powerful. It produces *energy*. Our creative spirit can generate a tremendous blast of force that, when added to our manifesting efforts, will ensure the accomplishment of our individual goals and intentions.

It's time you discovered and accepted your creative gifts. All of us have this ability. Some people have more talent than others but all of us, at one time or another, have demonstrated a knack for something. Your forte might not be in the fine arts, such as painting, sculpting, writing, dance, music, or theater, but you might be great at needlecrafts, designing, pottery, ceramics, sewing, or you just simply have a great eye for color. In this chapter, we will explore some of these abilities, and I'll tell you how you can best use them to draw whatever you want into your life. Get ready to get your hands dirty. Using these talents is productive, gratifying, and lots of fun.

So You're All Thumbs?

Let us start with the basics, for those of us who have not really been aware of our creative selves. If you feel you are all thumbs with hands-on projects, you may be wrong. Hands-on does not always mean making something out of nothing with your hands. It means you are able to fashion an expression of your inner being in such a way that it brings enjoyment to yourself and creates meaning for you. Notice I said you, not others. Art is very personal. The artist works for his or her own gratification, not anyone else's. Artists work because they have to. They are compelled to release their drive and energy in a sometimes familiar and sometimes abstract form. It is a cathartic blast of energy, meant to gratify the sender of that energy.

Your artistic expression, through whatever medium it is generated, can send such a powerful message because it comes from your inner depths, the part of you that is in direct communication with God. It is a dynamic and vital part of who you are. Think of it as pent-up energy, like the air in a champagne bottle that is waiting for the chance to blow the cork right into space.

You are innately creative. It is a quality you were born with. Expressing your creativity is a matter of simply deciding to use it. I encourage my more reluctant students to draw upon their creative energy in basic and uncompli-cated ways. Even if you can only draw stick figures, you can use that form to help you visualize your desires.

For instance, if it is a relationship you want, draw a man stick figure, with his little skinny arm reaching for the little skinny arm of a woman stick figure. Draw big smiles on their faces. Go back to kindergarten in a way, and let your imagination run wild. Put your stick people on a beach if that's what you enjoy, or in a home. Your drawing may look horrible to the trained eye, but no one but you is going to see it. Have fun. Then keep your picture with your rit-ual items and have it handy to gaze upon every day for inspiration and focus as you wait for your relationship to materialize in your life.

If money is your desire, draw a big dollar bill. Color it with crayons—noth-ing fancy is necessary. What is your image of abundance? Maybe you see money growing on trees. Put it there in your picture. Or you might envision boatloads of cash, so draw them. If you make mistakes, so what? Your work is for your eyes only. Get all those seemingly crazy thoughts on paper, because it is that free-spirited energy that can help to change your life.

Another way for the inexperienced creator to express and focus this impor-tant energy is to write. Get an inexpensive spiral notebook and pour out your thoughts and feelings about what you are trying to manifest. The journal you are using for the exercises in this book is a good place to write. Or you can buy a sketchbook so you can write and doodle in the same book, maybe adding colored inks. Dedicate a notebook to your creativity, and don't use it for any other purpose but manifesting. That will contain the energy and keep your thoughts from becoming scattered. Write your thoughts every day, or when-ever the spirit moves you.

Another form of written expression takes your creativity a bit further. You can write your own scripts to use as tools to manifest. For example, you might be involved in an unhealthy relationship and you want it to heal. Write an imaginary movie scene, changing the outcome as you would like it to be. Start with a stage direction like, "Camera pans across the front of a beautiful suburban home. The door is open to reveal a loving couple, holding hands as they exit to their car. They are off on a second honeymoon."

You can even write the dialogue to your script. Like so:

JOHN: Mary, I love you more than anything. Marry me, now!

MARY: Oh, John, you are the man of my dreams. The answer is yes, yes, yes!

(Ad nauseam, but you get the idea.) Write the corniest stuff if you like, whatever expresses your needs and wants. Don't worry about correct usage, punctuation, or spelling. The Big English Teacher in the Sky is not going to grade this paper! Enjoy, and feel the energy build.

Others who have trouble expressing their creativity, if not interested in drawing or writing, can do it through a visual process. I find that when I am confused or anxious, I enjoy a stroll through our neighborhood shopping mall. My intention is not to buy, but to look. The color and stimulation all around lift my spirits and clear my head. In like manner, you might choose to create color around you to stimulate and focus your energy. Buy flowers in the shades that express your feelings about your particular intention, and keep them on your altar. You might choose pink roses to draw love. But if yellow roses feel better to you, than get those. Don't be tied to society's definitions. Define your life and express yourself in your own style.

Paint your walls. Yes, that's right. Slap some color up there that sends a message to the Universe. If you want money, paint the wall green. If you don't want to ruin the expensive paint job you just commissioned, splash some colors on a piece of watercolor paper or canvas board. The paints, paper, and board are available at any craft store and will fit anyone's budget. No brush? Finger-paint! The point is, don't be limited. Let your imagination run wild. Try it. As you paint, you will feel an incredible release. That's the ammunition we need to give our manifesting the shot it needs.

Can't sing, but love music? Use it to express yourself. Sing in the shower. Pick a tune that embodies the essence of what you're trying to manifest. Belt it out! Sing in the car (those other drivers will never know). You'll just look silly, but who cares? You will feel great!

Gotta dance, but have two left feet? Lock the door and go for it. The music you choose should be upbeat and have a quick rhythm. Dance your pants off! Take a tip from the whirling dervishes, a religious sect who twirl in a circle to express their spirituality. Play that Beatles song, "Money, That's What I Want," if money is what you want. Keep it light and have a good time.

Are you a great chef, or do you just enjoy cooking? Okay, now you are probably thinking, "How can I possibly manifest by cooking?" Well, you can help your manifesting along with food, and it is very easy. Bake. Bake cookies in the shape of your desire. Fashion hearts for love, rectangles for money. Use food coloring to dye them to the appropriate colors. Use icing to write words or draw pictures to make the project suit your personal intention. Do the same with a cake, and frost it in such a way as to express your desire. Then eat those goodies with relish knowing you have reinforced your message for the Universe.

You are probably feeling as though this is crazy advice but I'll tell you, it works. The more you declare yourself through creative means, the closer you get to your goals. Who said manifesting had to be stodgy or dull?

Crafty Advice

Crafts are another way of generating our spiritual creative energy. A stroll through a neighborhood craft shop can boggle the mind. There are so many available ways to pour out your creative juices, from needlepoint to candle making. In fact, let's talk about those two.

If stitchery attracts you, find a needlepoint, crewel, or cross-stitch kit with a picture or saying that embodies the essence of the intention you are trying to manifest. If none moves you, design your own. Avid crafters know that you can always design your own projects, and the tools are easy to get and use. As you work on the project, do so as a form of meditation. This craft can be very relaxing. The process of stitching can soothe the mind, and you can focus on the reason you are making it. It might end up as a pillow, which you can put in your bedroom or on your couch reminding you of your desire and reinforcing the message to the Universe. I have a needlepoint pillow in my car with a personal message written on it. Each time I gaze at it, I feel energized and motivated to move toward my goal.

Making candles is an ancient craft regaining popularity today. Craft stores have these supplies readily available, and they are relatively inexpensive. Fashioning your own candles is one of the most sacred crafts you can choose. The candle, as you know, represents the fire element in the Universe, and you may burn your personally made candles as part of your ritual. This is the one craft that can be immediately and directly connected to your manifesting, as an active part of your process. You may add oils, flowers, or trinkets to the candles to represent your intention, enhancing their energy. You can even write messages on your personally made candles to carry your thoughts to the Universe. With a pen knife, carve a word into the candle, such as Prosperity, Love, Abundance, or Health. Whatever word or phrase that applies to your intention would be appropriate. Even the colors of the wax may be chosen for their significance to you. Candles are easy to make and pack a lot of power.

Ceramics, woodworking, and modeling with clay or other media are all great crafts you can enjoy that will assist you in attracting your desires. You can mold a clay statue, whittle a wooden ritual tool, or paint a ceramic piece that embodies your intention, all of which can be placed on your altar, in various parts of your home, or in your office to remind you daily of your goal.

If none of the crafts I have mentioned spark your interest, take a trip to a craft store and let something "speak" to you. As you walk down the aisles, meditate by clearing your mind. Ask your higher self to direct you to what you need. Let your intuition guide you and trust that Spirit will lead you to your perfect craft. You'll know what it is because you will have a reaction to it. Go with your first impressions, and don't censor them with logic. You might think, "That looks like fun, but it's probably too hard for me because I'm all thumbs." Now, that is negative thinking. Instead think, "That looks like fun. I'll get it and give it my best shot." *That* is the kind of thinking that gets you everything you ever wanted.

For the Experienced Artist

Some of us have been blessed with great talent. If you are one of these people, you already know the joy of expressing your heart on canvas or paper, in sculpture, or performance. You have felt the release of this spiritual energy and understand its power. Experienced artists, amateur or professional, understand the complete ecstasy of immersing oneself in a project and losing all track of time and reality. When we are thoroughly engaged in an activity that resonates with our spirit, the very core of who we are, that energy overpowers all else. We are focused and intently concentrating to the extent that we forget the everyday world and are lifted to a place within us that is inexplicable and totally peaceful.

As we create from this sacred place within us, we truly connect with the Godforce, the Source of our being. Any artist will tell you that being in that space in their consciousness, the creative mind, is the most wonderful, gratifying feeling they have ever experienced. It is beyond all time and space. At that moment, their creative expression is the reason for their existence, and drives their art forward in the face of all adversity. It is true love. How many rich artists do you know? I know very few. Most are struggling but do so willingly, because this feeling is so precious to them and worth any amount of sacrifice. When the artist is truly in sync with their art, they are directly communing with Spirit, so the struggle ends and success is inevitable. The act of artistic expression, the moment they put pen to paper or brush to canvas, they feel as if they are walking in the company of angels. This is very powerful energy, to say the least.

If you are one of these artists, use your art to assist you in getting your heart's desires. An artist myself, I have used music, theater, writing, and painting to send my messages to the Universe in my own unique way, and have been very blessed in the process. I have written songs, performed theatrical dramatic monologues, written poetry, and done abstract painting all based on the single intention I am trying to manifest. It is not necessary to share this sacred art with anyone else. It is just necessary to do it. That is enough to carry your message to the Universe. If you have a true talent and do not use it for sacred means, you do yourself and your spirit a great injustice. The more involved in art you are, the more power you have. Use it, and you will find remarkable events and people coming into your life.

You *must*, of course, use your art in your manifesting process, if what you are trying to draw into your life is related to your art in any way. If you want your paintings to be in a gallery or show, use them as part of your ritual to help manifest it. Keep one or two paintings near your altar as you meditate and visualize them in the gallery of your choice, already hanging on the walls. See people walking by and admiring them, and see yourself cashing a check for a painting that was purchased from the show.

Musicians should place the sheet music of a song they wish to be published or recorded under a candle during their manifesting ritual. They should also sing their affirmation or play an instrument to enhance the energy of the moment.

Whatever your talent, draw it into your sacred practice in any way that feels comfortable. Come on, you're an artist. For you, this is a piece of cake! The more of yourself you employ in your manifesting, the stronger your message.

The Spiritual Artist in You

The power within us to create beauty and art is one of the most important gifts we humans have been given by the Universe. It is no accident that we have the capacity to do these wonderful things. You have only to look at the sculptures of Botticelli, the paintings of da Vinci, hear the music of Beethoven, and read the texts of Shakespeare to know we are remarkable beings. This ability to create the environment around us belongs to us all, not just the great masters. They serve as encouragement and role models for us, to inspire us to use the talent we have been given to the best of our ability, whatever its extent. This energy of the human spirit—its ability to fashion art and beauty, to make something from nothing—can change the world. Use yours to change your life.

CHAPTER 12

Being Grateful

*A*bove all else, we must learn that everything that comes to us is a gift. We already have so much to be grateful for. Our lives are already full of wonderful gifts from the Universe, yet we seem to always need more. There never seems to be enough money in our pockets, leisure time to enjoy, good trusting friends, and on and on it goes. What is enough? When do we have all that we need and desire? These questions are simple, yet profound. The answer lies deep within us. In truth, we are already enough. We already have everything we need to make us happy. In short, we don't really need anything.

You are probably thinking, "If that's so, then why did she write this book?" Good question. We already have everything we need, *in spiritual form.* In material form, though, there is much to be desired, and that is why I wrote this book. We need to have a comfortable physical existence to fulfill our individual life purpose and to live the blissful life that God intended for us. Our spirit is already fulfilled because the Source, the Godforce, the Creator, is perfect and has all it needs, always. We are the walking embodiment of the Creator on this Earth, and that part of us is perfect and totally fulfilled. It needs nothing. The closer we get to our enlightenment, meaning the more we grow in spiritual understanding, the stronger our relationship becomes with our Universe, our Source, and the less we need. But we are not fully spiritual beings, totally enlightened. We are not God, in its highest sense.

Our humanness has certain requirements for living on this planet. These requirements, or needs, come with the territory. Physical existence bears the necessity of getting along in a materialistic society. To quote a book I once read, "Even mystics have to pay bills."

It would be wonderful to live on an Earth that was as full and lush as the biblical accounts of the Garden of Eden—a special heaven where there is no pain or struggle, and no one wants for anything. The reality of our lives is quite different. We do suffer pain, struggle, sickness, heartbreak, and all the ills of this material world, but these difficulties are part of the glorious experience of life. God put us here, and we agreed to come, to be a walking, breathing expression of Itself. The Creator sees Itself in us. We exist so that God can observe Itself. Humanity is God's little diversion, if you will. Of course, an energy as vast as God doesn't really *need* anything, and didn't really need to create us at all. God, in Its loving goodness, created us to give us a very important gift. In bestowing that gift upon Its creations, God can see Itself at work. This gift is life.

This gift of life is precious and priceless. It was given in love and with the greatest of intentions. We have been given life so that we can express God on Earth. This expression means that we are here to do God's work. In that very expression, living a positive, loving, and joyful life in service to the Creator and its creations, we show our gratitude. So, in our everyday living, as we conduct ourselves impeccably, making every effort to act in our highest good and the highest good of all those we encounter, we give thanks. Our life, lived well, is an expression of gratitude to our maker.

Gratitude is the greatest gift we can give to Spirit. To live an exemplary life in God's grace, cherishing all its creatures and creations, is the reason we were put here in the first place. We already have what we need. The part of us that is God within us needs nothing. The human part of us, though, needs much to conduct God's business on Earth, and simply to keep our bodies alive to do the work. That is one of the many reasons we learn to speak to God in prayer and affirmation, so that It can support our functioning on this planet. We need God to assist us in doing Its work, much like a good manager needs his employees to do the work of the company. It is up to the manager to keep his employees happy, fulfilled, and content. If he is good at that challenge, his workers will reward him with loyalty, hard work, and gratitude.

A loving and benevolent Universe that needs nothing in and of Itself is perfectly happy to give us all that we need to continue Its work here. The struggle and pain we may endure in our lives is not planned by God. Rather, we have planned and created it as lessons to be learned in order to know God better. Our darkness, our difficult times, our mistakes, and our painful situations are all necessary so that the human part of us can appreciate the God in ourselves and in all energies of the Universe.

Just Ask

The way to get everything we ever wanted is to accept that we deserve it. We must know and understand that God wants us to be happy, to prosper, and to live in abundance. A loving energy such as God would not inflict pain. We do that ourselves. This benevolent energy of Spirit provides us with all that we desire to grow closer to It, and to help others grow closer to It as well—but there is one catch. We must ask for what we want. God will support us if we make our needs and desires clear and known to It. It follows, then, that the only response of a loving God is unlimited and unconditional support. God will give you what you ask for if you ask in a selfless and grateful way.

When we ask God to fulfill our desires, we must be thankful first for what we already have. That is easy. Our attitude must be positive, and we must truly believe that life is more than enough to be grateful for. Anything else we may receive during this life in the way of material possessions, loving relationships, emotional happiness, etc., is just gravy—the icing on the cake—and we can live without it all because ultimate satisfaction and joy, God, is already within and a part of us.

Asking for what we need demonstrates to God that we are grateful for the help we are in the process of receiving. Making a request of the Universe sends the message that we trust in its love and support. This positive energy invokes a positive reaction, and we receive what we want. Have you ever asked someone for help and they respond by saying, "Thanks for coming to me, I appreciate your trust"? In much the same way, the Universe appreciates your gesture of faith and rewards you.

Gratitude Is a Magnet

Being grateful for our lives must be a strong driving force for us in order to manifest our desires. Gratitude comes first, not the other way around. Yes, our mothers taught us to say, "Thank you," when we received a gift or generous gesture, so we were conditioned to believe that the grateful acknowledgment follows rather than precedes the gift. As adults, we must come to realize that we receive gifts *because we are thankful,* and that energy of appreciation is what attracted the gift in the first place.

For example, we enjoy giving gifts to people who truly enjoy receiving them and who react in complementary ways. They get excited and do a lot of "ooh-ing" and "ah-ing" and gushing over them. They even use and enjoy the gifts we give them. On the contrary, we really dislike giving gifts to people who always return or exchange them, give them away, or don't get very excited about receiving them at all. Which one of these two types of people is really *attracting* the gift? The one who has a basic sense of gratitude. We know this type of person will be appreciative, so we give them a gift. They are gratitude magnets. The attitude precedes the action.

This whole attraction process is most often working on a spiritual level unbeknownst to our conscious mind. A person lives thankfully on an invisible level in their thoughts and feelings. Remember, thoughts are powerful things, and their messages are silently working throughout our lives, broadcasting positive or negative vibrations all around us. Did you ever get a gift unexpectedly, when there was no occasion for it? Someone sensed your receptivity and was moved on a psychic level to show you their love, respect, or appreciation. Your grateful nature inspired a generous response.

This grateful receptivity works as a manifesting magnet. When we let God know that we are ready to receive whatever comes our way, through our positive daily statements and thoughts of thanks for life itself, and the many blessings we already possess, we open the floodgates of God's generosity and love. Negativity and ingratitude slams them shut. Negativity creates distance from God, and things don't come as easily to us as we'd like. A positive, loving attitude is crucial to our receptivity to all that is wonderful in the Universe.

The Universal Law of Circulation

A very important metaphysical principle exists in the Universe. You are familiar with it, I am sure. If you have had a traditional religious Christian upbringing, you might remember this biblical quote: "As you give, so shall you receive." I am not big on quoting the Bible, but this statement is an absolute truth. Everyday I see the results of this basic tenet of life. In metaphysics, this principle of giving in order to receive is called the Universal Law of Circulation.

The word "circulation" implies that something is going round and round. Whether it be money, love, or good will, whatever you spread around is going to come back to you. Think about that when you spread gloom and doom. In order to be on the receiving end of our desires, we must spread around to others *exactly* what we want. In addition, we must do it with a grateful heart. Then the circle will be complete when our desire matches or is in sync with the desires of the others involved in our intention. All of this will be happening on an invisible, vibratory level. We are, in effect, circulating our energy when we voice our clear intention to the Universe and do all we can to attract it.

We can see that the Law of Circulation is working in our lives when, after we have made our desires known to the Universe, synchronistic events begin to happen. Shortly thereafter, our requests are materialized into our world. Giving to others the very thing that we intend to draw into our life starts a psychic chain reaction in the Universe. Our gift multiplies as it is spread from person to person and then returns to us multiplied.

You need not, nor should not, tell everyone what you are manifesting. Spread your intention in subtle ways. For instance, if you wish to become prosperous, or you want the flow of money to increase in your life, you must give it away. Of course, you must not make yourself penniless in the process, but rather you should portion a generous amount and give it to those in need and to the place or person who teaches you and inspires your spiritual growth, such as your church or spiritual mentor. These people and organizations, because they are spiritually oriented, will surely spread that money around to others so, according to the Law of Circulation, that's as good as money in the bank! If you give your money to those who would hoard it, don't expect to get any back, let alone a multiplied return!

Are you getting this? I hope so. Understanding this law is crucial to your manifesting. I include it here, at the end of the book, so that you will remember it. We usually remember the last thing we read. I'm also taking into account those folks who open the book and flip to read the ending first. If that's what you did, you now need to read the whole book to see how the principle of manifesting is built upon this premise. No cheating!

Don't Give to Get

Having said all that, there is one little caveat I need to tell you about. Giving must be done with a grateful heart, and you must give *without expecting to receive.* If your only motivation to give money to your church is to make a show of your gratitude and get you more money back, forget it. The Universe is wise to you. It knows you are not totally good-intentioned, and you can kiss your money goodbye. If this sounds like something you've done, you'd better say plenty of affirmations to remove greed and fear from your mentality.

Selfless giving clearly demonstrates to the Universe that you are thankful for the opportunity to live and thrive and, more importantly, you show that you want the best for others, too. Remember, God put us here to help others as well as ourselves. The Universe perceives your sincerity and generosity, and gives you more reason to be generous by sending more opportunities for money to come into your life. This response motivates you to keep the manifesting ball rolling. By helping others, you have helped yourself.

Before you begin to receive, you must trust that the Universe will support you. You must believe that what you want is possible, and that it can surely be yours. Being grateful for God's help and support restores your confidence and removes all your fear. This strength guides you to spread your intention to the right people, who will respond to it on both a conscious and subconscious level and return the favor, multiplied. Giving with gratitude of your energy, money, time, or love circulates on the unseen levels of the Universe in such a positive way that miraculous things happen. Whatever you want comes to you without resistance or struggle.

Contentment Breeds Power

Your gratitude is clear to the Universe when you live in a state of contentment. Being truly spiritually content should be an important goal in your life. Spiritual contentment means that you are emotionally satisfied with the material possessions you have and the quality of your life at any given moment.

Contented people do have dreams, you know. They have goals and aspirations, too, but they are perfectly happy with the status quo. We sometimes call them "well-adjusted." These balanced souls are able to wait patiently for their future to unfold. It is not that they don't try to get everything they want, it is just that they don't get anxious about it. They put their messages out into the cosmos and are calm and sure that their requests will be heard. No nervous breakdowns here!

To be one of these beautiful people takes effort. The content among us manage to stay that way in the face of adversity. They can maintain their balance regardless of the situation or chaos that occurs around them. These are the folks that don't fall apart when they lose their jobs, suffer through the death of a loved one, or are victims of one of life's physical misfortunes. Think of the actor Christopher Reeve and his spiritual strength throughout his battle with full paralysis after a riding accident. He is content with his situation but determined to help himself and others by supporting the efforts to find a cure for spinal injuries. I was amazed when I heard him say in an interview, that this is the hand that life dealt him, so he was going to play it out as best he could. Since that time, he has written a book, appeared on countless television programs, directed a film, and touched the lives of millions of people. His contentment has made him more powerful than ever.

The serenity that comes only from a place of contentment within us is very powerful. Our quiet strength sends the ultimate message to the Universe that we are most thankful for who we are right now and the course our life has taken. This invisible force that we project silently radiates within our world and attracts more of the same to us. Remarkably, the less we do and the more satisfied we are, the faster our prayers are answered.

Believe and Affirm

A simple, steadfast confidence in the benevolence and generosity of the Universe expressed as gratitude in prayer or affirmation is the most powerful tool we humans possess. With it we cannot lose, nor can we ever be ignored. Our belief in the power to make our dreams come true through the daily display of gratitude renews our spirit and enhances our lives.

You cannot reach your manifesting goals alone, without the help of Spirit. A day should not go by without our offering some acknowledgment of our Creator, the source of our good fortune. Continued spiritual renewal is vitally necessary to maintain your abundance and to keep getting what you ask for so that you'll never be without, or experience lack again.

To end this chapter, I'd like to share one of my favorite quotations with you. These are the words of Benjamin Franklin. They were spoken in Philadelphia, Pennsylvania, on June 28, 1787, at a debate in the Constitutional Convention. It seems Franklin was advocating that each session of the Convention begin with prayers, "imploring the assistance of Heaven, and its blessings on our deliberations."

> I have lived, Sir, a long time, and the longer I live, the more convincing proofs I see of this truth—*that God governs in the affairs of men.* And if a sparrow cannot fall to the ground without his notice, is it probable that an empire can rise without his aid?

I wish I'd said that.

CHAPTER 13

Words for the Wise

Now that you know everything there is to know about using your psychic common sense to get everything you ever wanted, I'll send you on your way to a lifetime of fulfillment and bliss with a collection of affirmations that work. Earlier in the book, you learned to write your own affirmations, and they will be effective because they come from your heart. But for the folks who have trouble putting thoughts on paper, the following affirmations may be substituted for those of your own design.

Included in this chapter are affirmations for drawing anything and everything, or anyone, for that matter, into your life. This is a very comprehensive list of positive and powerful thoughts. Use them as a guide. I have broken down the list into two categories—Preparation Affirmations and Manifesting Affirmations. The Preparation Affirmations are meant to help you prepare for manifesting by removing doubt, fear, confusion, and the like. Use these clearing affirmations before you begin manifesting if you have some blocks or just need a dose of some spiritual confidence. The second category, Manifesting Affirmations, are to be used directly for attracting a specific intention or essence.

I have simplified the process of writing affirmations for you, but you will still have to add some elements to them. Refer back to chapter 4, "Tapping Into Your Power," and the section on "Say It." Add the elements I have eliminated. I did not include the complete affirmations here, to avoid repetition. An affirmation will work even in its simplest form but, if you are a beginner, take care not to eliminate any of the elements. Rewrite these affirmations in the style used in chapter 4, rewording when necessary. When you are an old hand at manifesting, you will probably be skilled enough to add the missing ingredients from memory. *Whatever you do, don't forget the gratitude part! The word "thanks" has to be in there.*

Let us take the first affirmation listed under "Preparation Affirmations," and rewrite it by adding the necessary elements.

"I accept joy, power, love, happiness, money, abundance, and good health into my life."

*I thank the Universe (God/Goddess/my higher self/the Source/
All There Is) and I accept joy, power, love, happiness, money,
abundance, and good health into my life. They are already mine,
and come to me in a safe and loving way, according to divine
will and the free will of all concerned. And so it is.*

You can see how the intention fits into the basic format of the affirmation. Let's try another one.

"I accept a new loving attitude, and joyfully receive all the blessings of the Universe."

I thank the Universe (God/Goddess/my higher self/the Source/
All There Is) as I accept a new loving attitude, and joyfully
receive all the blessings of the Universe. They are already mine,
and come to me in a safe and loving way, according to divine
will and the free will of all concerned. And so it is.

Now, we will rewrite a specific manifesting affirmation. This one has a slightly different form. Use whatever is comfortable for you.

"All the money I need to pay off my current credit card debt comes to me now."

All the money I need to pay off my current credit card debt comes
to me now. I thank the Universe for this, which is already mine
and comes to me in a safe and loving way, according to divine
will and the free will of all concerned. And so it is.

There are many schools of thought as affirmations go. Some metaphysicians simply use the single sentence. If you wish, you may do so. I have found it more effective, when first beginning your manifesting, to include all the necessary elements, particularly protection and gratitude. That is not to say that you will not receive your intention if you leave them out. You probably will. I like the insurance of knowing I have sufficiently thanked God for Its intervention and that what I desire comes to me safely. If you simply ask for all the money you need to pay off your credit cards, you will get it, but the money might come to you in an undesirable way, such as an inheritance due to the death of a parent or loved one. I know someone who requested a new car radio, free of charge. A few days later, thieves broke into her car and stole the old one! She received her new radio, paid for by her auto insurance. It was free, but came to her the hard way. She learned her lesson and, after hearing that story, so did I.

I'm sure you now understand how to adjust these affirmations, and how very important the correct wording is, not to mention a positive attitude, which is absolutely necessary to propel the energy of your desires forward. Let your intuition assist you in choosing and writing a particular affirmation. It is wiser than logic. All of the following affirmations listed have worked either for myself or for my students. Anyone can use them to achieve success.

When you are ready to begin, clear your mind, take a few deep breaths, and just relax. Forget about the clothes that have to be washed and the dinner that needs to be cooked, and take a little time for yourself. Start today to create the life you want.

Preparation Affirmations

Acceptance

I accept joy, power, love, happiness, money, abundance, and good health into my life.

I accept a new loving attitude, and joyfully receive all the blessings of the Universe.

Action

I act on my loving intentions and move through difficulties with ease.

Attraction

Today I attract all that I need to create abundance in my life.
The power is within me.

Balance and Flow

My entire energy is in balance and harmony with all of life.
I flow with the process of life, and all of its events and happenings
strengthen me. I am renewed, healthy, and happy.

Blocks

I release blocks, pain, and negativity in this current life,
and connect with my greatest good.

Change

Change is normal. I cope with the changes life
has to offer easily and without struggle.

Ego

My ego is healthy and vital, and under control.

Fear and Doubt

I recognize that, at times, I am fearful. At that moment,
I breathe deeply and ask the Universe for guidance.

Fear is a figment of my imagination. From now on,
I choose only joy and fulfillment.

I face my life without fear or doubt.

Higher Power

I accept and thank the wisdom within as it guides me through my
life and leads me to the fulfillment of my heart's desires.

I ask for higher guidance to assist me in creating what I want.

I clear my mind and allow the messages of Spirit
to flow through me.

Intuition

I pay more attention to my intuition than my logical mind,
because it is always accurate.

Peace

I live in a state of peace, joy, and light.

*Peace is the normal way of life for me. Each day, I begin by
affirming my eternal peace and harmony with life
and all things within it.*

Positive Energy

Each day I create positive energy, circumstances, and events.

Problems

*I allow my problems to work themselves out
without pain and struggle.*

Protection

*I draw a circle of white light and protection around me
as I open to the energy of the Universe.*

Psychic Self

*I open to my psychic self. All information comes to me freely
from Spirit, and I am ready to accept it.*

Receiving

I am ready and open to receive my desires. I am in the perfect place and have all that it takes to accomplish my goals.

I create all that I need and want. Everything comes easily to me. I am living in a constant state of abundance.

I am open and ready for the abundance of the Universe to manifest in my life.

Responsibility

I know that I am here by my own design, and I take full responsibility for my life.

I have the free will, sense of responsibility, and spiritual integrity I need to create a loving and joyful life.

Spiritual Assistance

I welcome and honor the presence of my helpers in spirit, angels, and spirit guides. I have divine help as I go through this life.

I am never alone. I am always in the company of angels.

When I need help or guidance, I just ask my angels and they answer me.

*When I need help or guidance, I just ask my spirit guide
and it answers me.*

Spiritual Goals

*It is easy for me to set spiritual goals. I am clear in my mind that
all that occurs or will occur in my life has spiritual meaning.*

*As I set goals for my spiritual growth, I am confident
they will be achieved.*

Struggle

*All forms of struggle are released from my consciousness
and my life. All is well and working in my highest good.*

Universal Power

*I am a powerful being and within me
is a source greater than I can imagine.*

*When I feel weak or unstable, I remember that the strength
of the Universe is within me, and the full sense of my power
and being are restored.*

The Universe is one divine energy from which all things manifest.

I am one with the Whole. All energies are my energy.

All levels of possibility are available to me. The Universe
is limitless, and so is my reality.

Wisdom

I am wise and make sound choices.

My knowledge, skills, and talents help to make this lifetime
a loving, abundant, prosperous, and fulfilling one.

Manifesting Affirmations

All-purpose
These first affirmations are all-purpose and can be used for any intention.
Insert yours on the blank line.

I focus my energy on _____.
I draw it to me now.

I (draw or remove) _____
(to or from) my life, now.

All the energies in the Universe help me to draw
_____ into my life.

I thank Spirit for sending _____ into my life.

The following two affirmations cover everything in general.

I understand and am clear. I know what I need and want
in my life, and it all comes to me now.

All that I need I receive through Spirit.

The affirmations listed here are for very specific requests. Some will require your inserting a word or phrase to reflect your special intention.

Addictions

I release my addiction to _____
(smoking, alcohol, drugs, sex, etc.) now. I am free
from this dependency forever.

Car purchase/sale

I am the proud owner of a brand-new car. This (you may add
the model, year, make, color, etc., if you like, or just insert the
word "car") _____ comes to me now.

My car is sold. The perfect buyer is coming to me now, and my
car is sold for the exact price I desire, _____
(you can actually put the price here, or just end the affirmation
at the word "desire"). (You can also use this affirmation to buy or
sell anything. Just replace the word "car" with your specific item.)

Confidence

I exude confidence. I face all situations with poise and grace.
My self-confidence and faith in my ability is strong
and never wavers.

Court case

I am winning this court case. Victory is mine because I have
acted in everyone's highest good. My lawyer is honest and
trustworthy, and acts in my best interest.

Debt

I am free of all debt. My (credit card bills, loan, mortgage, etc.)
_____ is paid.

I happily bless and pay all my bills. Debt leaves my life, now.

Decisions

I make important decisions easily.

My decisions are always strong, sound, clear,
perfect for me, and in my highest good.

Fame

I am famous, and enjoy all the blessings that come along with it.

*I use my fame responsibly to help the world,
its people, and its important causes.*

I always give back to the Universe in loving ways.

Financial independence

I am financially independent.

All the money I need is mine, exactly when I need it.

I have all the money I will ever need or want.

Friends

*I attract loving, generous, spiritual, trustworthy,
and loyal friends into my life.*

My friends always act in my highest good.

*My friends and I enjoy and share life together,
in fun and joyful ways.*

Happiness

Happiness is a part of my life now and always.

*I attract happiness in the form of positive people,
situations, and events that enter my life.*

Harmony at work

My work environment is positive and harmonious.

I get along with my coworkers very well.

My employer (boss) is fair and respectful.

Healing the body/perfect health

*My _____ is healed. I am restored to perfect
health now. Dis-ease is gone from my body and my life.*

Heart condition

I have a perfect, strong, and healthy heart.

All dis-ease, pain, fear, and anger is released from my heart.

My heart is healed.

My heart is strong and functions perfectly within my body.

Impending surgery

My surgery goes well, and I am divinely protected through it.

My doctors are skilled, careful, and respectful of me.

My operation is a total success, and I heal quickly.

Incurable disease

*This disease leaves my body now, and I have
released the need for it in my life.*

*I thank this disease for helping me to grow in Spirit
as I free it from my body and am healed.*

I am healed and in perfect health.

Intuition/psychic development

My intuition and psychic ability develop easily.

I open and cultivate my inner power.

Job/career/employment

The new job (career) I seek is now mine. It is right and perfect for me, and comes to me easily.

Lack

Abundance and prosperity replace lack in my life, and I always have all that I need.

Loneliness

My life is full of wonderful people who are there for me whenever I need them.

Lost articles

The _____ I lost has now been found, and is restored into my life.

Love/mate/companionship

The love (mate, companionship, etc.) I seek is now mine. He (she) is right and perfect for me, and has been divinely selected and sent to me now.

Money/prosperity

Money flows freely into my life.

The Universe (God/Goddess, etc.) prospers my life now.

I am prosperous, and my prosperity is unlimited.

Money is attracted to me now.

All the money I need is mine now.

Money comes to me easily and without struggle.

The money I need for _____
comes into my life now in the amount of
_____ or more.

New life

I release my old way of life and open to the joy
and wonder of the new life ahead of me.

Opportunity

Opportunity is all around me. New opportunities are opening
up to me now, and I accept them into my life.

Overweight

I now release my excess weight.

My body is beautiful and at its perfect weight and size.

My life is in control and in perfect balance.

*No matter what I eat I lose weight because the need
for the extra weight has left my life.*

Pain

*Pain has left my _____ (body, mind,
heart, etc., or write in a specific body part) and my life,
and I am totally pain-free.*

Pain is gone from my life, my body, and my consciousness.

Passing a test/interview

*I pass this test (interview) easily. My mind is clear,
I am calm and confident, and success is mine.*

Patience

*Patience is now a part of my life. My serenity and
peace of mind are obvious to me and to others.*

Performing

I am totally calm and at peace when I perform.
My talent is at its best at all times.

Pregnancy

My partner and I are very fertile, and we conceive a child easily.

My body responds well to nature, and I have
an easy and comfortable pregnancy.

Public speaking

It is easy for me to speak in public, and I am calm
and poised before an audience.

I have complete confidence in my ability to speak in public
because my audience is attentive and receptive to my talk.

Publishing

My book (article, story, etc.) is published now.

The opportunity to share my thoughts
with the world comes to me easily.

I have the perfect publisher, and together
we are extremely successful.

Reconciliation

My _____ (family, mother, father,
sister, friend, coworker, lover, etc.) and I are reconciled,
and our differences are resolved.

I understand and forgive my _____,
and he (she/they) does (do) the same for me,
and we get along well.

Sale/purchase of property

My _____ is sold. The perfect buyer (seller)
is coming to me now, and my _____ is sold
(purchased) for the exact price I desire, _____,
(you can actually put the price here, or just end the affirmation
at the word "desire") or that which is in the highest good
of all concerned.

Success

I live a totally successful life.

Success in my business affairs comes to me now.

My _____ (art, business, marriage,
relationship, partnership, etc.) is extremely successful,
and contributes to my spiritual good and
the betterment of humankind.

_____ is a completely successful year for me.

Vacation

A fulfilling, restful, and perfect vacation is awaiting me.

My vacation is full of rest and relaxation, and all plans go well,
without delays or problems.

I always travel in complete safety, protected by the Universe.

Writer's block

Thoughts, ideas, and words flow freely from
the Universe to my conscious mind.

Writing is a joy and I do it with love,
easily and without struggle.

Blessings to you. May this book and these positive, powerful thoughts help to guide your way, and may you always get everything you ever wanted.

Go in light, love, and peace. And so it is!

Afterword

Okay, you've read the book, but should you have any lingering doubts about how well my method works, I've got a story to tell you that might eliminate those suspicions, once and for all.

Since moving to the beautiful Hudson Valley in upstate New York, I have had a dream. It seemed to me, that if one is so blessed to live near this great river, one should be able to see it. From the vantage point of Poughkeepsie, New York, the Hudson River is clean, relatively unpolluted and gorgeous. So, I decided that I'd better put my words into action to make my dream come true, of owning a home overlooking the Hudson.

I set out to manifest a townhouse with a view. Of course, I had to make some effort and take action, so I called several realtors and told them what I wanted. "You're never gonna find anything like that in your price range," they said, almost annoyed that I'd waste their time. I had faith, nonetheless, and pressed on. I called realtor Paula Sheedy who, in her unassuming way, agreed to help me. She didn't laugh when I told her how much I could afford, she actually took me seriously, and apologetically showed me the only thing she had, which was nothing short of a dump.

Well, I decided I wanted my home in July of 1999, began the search in August, and by the middle of September, we had found it! The ironic part of this story is that this townhouse had been sold just before I looked at it. Paula said, "Ooh, too bad you didn't call me sooner. I had something beautiful, in great shape right on the river, but it sold last week." I was calm. I thought to myself, "If I'm meant to have it, it'll be mine." About two weeks later, Paula called, excitement in her voice, to tell me that the deal fell through on the place and that if I wanted it I'd better get there, pronto!

I saw it that afternoon, and quickly made an offer. The sellers accepted it, but then another buyer came along and offered much more than I could afford. They decided to see which one of us would come up with more dough, and threw us into a bidding war. I just wouldn't play that game, because I still felt, "If I'm meant to have it, it'll be mine. It's in Spirit's hands now." I geared up for the disappointment, and to my amazement and hers, Paula called to tell me that the sellers went with me, even though it meant less money for them!

In my excitement, I didn't think about any future problems with the deal. All I could envision was that gorgeous view. Unforeseeably, my mortgage company appraised the property at $9,000 lower than our negotiated price. Now what? I figured that I lost it because I didn't have enough money to pay the difference between the appraised and asking prices, so, I reasoned that Spirit was either giving me a great bargain, or saving me from being taken. I affirmed again, "If I'm meant to have it, it'll be mine. It's in Spirit's hands now."

The sellers decided to put the place back on the market, and I took up the search once again, trusting that the Universe was in charge. After two weeks, Paula called to tell me that they decided to let me have it for a couple of thousand dollars over the appraised price. What? I couldn't believe my ears. How could this be? This was not just a bargain, it was a coup set up by the Universe to test my faith. I guess I passed. Whew!

So, my friends, as I write this, I am gazing out from my laptop at the majestic Hudson River. This morning, an energetic college rowing team sailed by, a determined little tugboat pulling a barge followed, and a laughing couple in a motorboat whizzed past. Across from my side of the river, a cargo train with a string of thirty or so cars, meandered down to some unknown destination, and I was lulled by the chug, chug, chugging, as it went by. Ah, life is good! Or, should I say, God is good!

My home didn't manifest into my life until after I wrote this book, so my editor, Becky Zins, suggested I tell you about it, here, as living proof that this method really works. Now, if you'll excuse me, I think I see a sailboat coming this way, and I want to relax, kick off my shoes, and watch the gentle billowing of its sails in the wind . . . (yawn)

When you manifest your desires using the techniques in this book, I would love to hear from you. Write me ℅ Llewellyn at the address stated in the "To Write to the Author" section at the beginning of this book. In your letter you may also request a list of my audiocassette lectures on positive spiritual living.

Thanks for reading, and God bless!

Dr. Adrian Calabrese

Glossary

Affirmations

Positive statements that inform the Universe/God of what we want to draw into our lives. Affirmations are crucial in attracting what we want because they embody our true intention and the essence of what we need or desire, and so they must be carefully worded. Once an affirmation is released it works as a magnet to draw our desires to us.

Altar

A dedicated space or table upon which we place sacred objects used to perform our manifesting rituals.

Angel

One of the most powerful loving energies in the Universe, assigned by God to protect and guide humans and all other forms of life. They are unseen forces that have never had a physical lifetime. Angels are the guardians of all life, and even guide us through and beyond our death.

Astral Plane

An unseen level of being or dimension that exists simultaneously with our physical plane. Souls and spirits are said to reside here after death, and communicate with us from this state. Also called the spirit plane.

Block

A negative thought, fear, or doubt that mentally stops us from getting what we want. Blocks occur within our subconscious mind and may be known or unknown to our conscious mind. It is important that we discover these blocks and release them in order to attract what we want.

Channel

A person who is able to sense unseen energies and discern messages from them. What distinguishes a channel from a medium or psychic is the channel's ability to allow a positive entity or personality from the spirit plane to use their mind and body as an instrument to deliver psychic messages. In other words, the entity is permitted to take over the body and literally speak through the channel.

Divine Plan

The set of lessons we choose to learn, or our predesigned plan for our current lifetime. We form the divine plan along with God while we are in spirit form, before we are born or reincarnate. We decide for ourselves who we will be, what lessons we will learn, and how we will learn them. It is our destiny.

Divine Will

A combination of what God wants for us and what we want for ourselves. Our will and the divine will are one and the same because God exists within us.

Energy

A source of unseen, usable power that exists in all things, animate and inanimate.

Free Will

Our God-given right to make any choice we wish, take any path we desire, and be whomever we want to be.

God/Spirit/Universe/ Greater or Higher Power/Goddess/All There Is

The Source of all creation—life itself. The perfect energy from which everything in the Universe was created. God is the beginning and the end, the all-good, all-loving energy that pervades the cosmos. It is an immanent, neutral Spirit energy that loves and supports Its creations. All life comes from It and returns to It. (My sincere attempt to describe the indescribable!)

Higher Consciousness

Also known as our higher self, spiritual self, intuition, or intuitive self, it is the part of us that is beyond our physical body, the God within, in direct contact with all the energies of the Universe. Our higher consciousness is our spirit, our soul. It is best to rely on this force within us since its prompting is always correct, very powerful, and guides us to our greater good.

Intention

The underlying reason why we do or do not do something. It can be positive, which will yield positive results, or negative, which will result in the opposite. Either way, our true intention determines the outcome of what we attract into our lives.

Karma

The universal law of cause and effect. We create positive or negative karma through our thoughts, words, and actions, and the way in which we live our life. Karma can bridge lifetimes and, when unresolved, can follow us through the ages and affect our future lives. Basically, karma means that the energy of whatever we do, think, or say comes back to us in some form. How we resolve or deal with it determines the positive or negative events, relationships, and happenings in our lifetime.

Lessons

All of the events of our lives, both good and bad, designed to help us learn to grow spiritually. Only when a lesson is learned may we move on. Lessons will repeat themselves, or negative events of our lives will grow in intensity, until we have realized, understood, and learned the lesson. At that point our soul will learn new lessons, enabling us to reach our highest spiritual clarity or potential—enlightenment, or oneness with God.

Life Purpose

The reason for reincarnating in this lifetime. The overall life purpose of humans is to serve God and each other. How we choose to do that is up to us.

We each have a distinct life purpose based upon our karma, talents, wants, and needs of this lifetime. The life purpose is individualized by our choices or the specific way in which we decide to serve God and humanity.

Manifesting

The ability to draw, attract, and make real in physical form our thoughts, wishes, and desires. Also known as demonstrating.

Meditation

A silent form of introspection, prayer, and relaxation. Generally one assumes a comfortable sitting position, closes the eyes, and allows all thoughts to leave the mind while concentrating on a peaceful idea or image, hence achieving an altered state of consciousness.

Metaphysics

The mystical study of the existence of all life energy within the Universe, both physical and beyond, and its relationship to God. This is a positive philosophy that recognizes humanity's unique nature embodying a mind, body, and spirit working together as a single unit yet connected to all life, helping humanity create a loving, abundant, peaceful existence in service to God, others, the Earth, and all its life forms.

Psychic Ability

Having the capacity to discern information from deeper levels of the mind or consciousness and other planes of existence. The person with a highly developed psychic sense can receive and send powerful messages in thought form.

Psychic Self

This is the part of the human mind that is open to the unseen energies of the Universe. Our psychic self can receive thoughts, pictures, and sounds from other planes of existence, and send strong messages to the Universe through positive intention and mental imaging.

Psychometry

The psychic ability to "read" the history of an object by holding it in the hands and mentally focusing on it.

Reincarnation

A belief that the soul can pass from one body to another after death, and live a new lifetime. Previous lifetimes are known as past lives. Information from these past lives can shed light on the karma and lessons carried over that have yet to be resolved in the current lifetime.

Ritual

A personal or public spiritual practice performed with regularity to worship, give thanks, or manifest by recognizing and honoring the existence of a higher power and its assistance in our lives.

Self-Hypnosis

The technique of putting oneself in a deep state of relaxation, enabling the mind to be receptive to a positive suggestion, thereby changing physical behavior and responses.

Spirit Guide

An energy entity existing on the astral plane whose function is to advise, guide, and assist humans in living a positive, abundant, and peaceful life. Spirit guides are energies that have lived in human form and have an agreement with a specific individual, made prior to reincarnation, to remain as a helper in spirit while the individual lives out a physical lifetime. Guides, as they are known, are our best friends in spirit, helping us get through the day-to-day struggles of life.

Synchronicity

A term coined by Carl Jung to describe the meaningful coincidences that occur in our lives. The term implies that the Universe is not random and that all things happen for a reason. Therefore, there really are no coincidences, only meaningful synchronicities happening just as they are meant to happen, in perfect order and in their perfect time.

Visualization

A form of mental imaging in which the mind forms pictures of its own creation. The images formed are powerful thoughts that can be used to attract what we want into our lives through manifesting. Visualization has also been used to help individuals achieve a personal best, find spiritual peace, or to heal the body of disease.

Bibliography

Ansari, Masud. *Modern Hypnosis: Theory and Practice.* Washington, D.C.: Mas-Press, 1991.

Belhayes, Iris with Enid. *Spirit Guides: We Are Not Alone.* San Diego, California: ACS Publications, Inc., 1985.

Burnham, Sophy. *A Book of Angels: Reflections on Angels Past and Present and True Stories of How They Touch Our Lives.* New York: Ballantine Books, 1990.

Chopra, Deepak. *Creating Affluence: Wealth Consciousness in the Field of All Possibilities.* San Rafael, California: New World Library, 1993.

Emery, Marcia. *Intuition Workbook: An Expert's Guide to Unlocking the Wisdom of Your Subconscious Mind.* Englewood Cliffs, New Jersey: Prentice Hall, 1994.

Hall, Calvin S. and Vernon J. Nordby. *A Primer of Jungian Psychology.* Ontario, Canada: New American Library, 1973.

Hanson, Virginia, Shirley Nicholson, and Rosemarie Stewart, eds. *Karma: Rhythmic Return to Harmony.* Wheaton, Illinois: Quest Books, 1990.

Hill, Napoleon. *Think and Grow Rich.* New York: Ballantine Books, 1960.

Melody. *Love Is in the Earth: A Kaleidoscope of Crystals.* Wheatridge, Colorado: Earth-Love Publishing House, 1991.

Mishlove, Jeffrey. *Roots of Consciousness: The Classic Encyclopedia of Consciousness Studies.* Tulsa, Oklahoma: Council Oak Books, 1993.

Murphy, Joseph. *The Cosmic Power Within You.* New York: MJF Books, 1968.

Pajeon, Kala and Ketz. *The Candle Magick Workbook.* New York: Citadel Press, 1991.

238

Stevens, Jose. *Tao to Earth: Michael's Guide to Relationships and Growth.* Santa Fe, New Mexico: Bear & Company, Inc., 1994.

Waldman, Mark. *The Way of Real Wealth: Creating a Future That Is Emotionally Satisfying, Spiritually Fulfilling, Financially Secure.* New York: HarperCollins, 1993.

Walker, Barbara G. *The Book of Sacred Stones: Fact and Fallacy In the Crystal World.* New York: HarperCollins, 1989.

Wilde, Stuart. *Affirmations.* Carlsbad, California: Hay House, Inc., 1987.

_____. *The Trick To Money Is Having Some.* Carlsbad, California: Hay House, Inc., 1995.

Index

Free Magazine

Read unique articles by Llewellyn authors, recommendations by experts, and information on new releases. To receive a **free** copy of Llewellyn's consumer magazine, *New Worlds of Mind & Spirit,* simply call 1-877-NEW-WRLD or visit our website at www.llewellyn.com and click on *New Worlds.*

LLEWELLYN ORDERING INFORMATION

Order Online:
Visit our website at www.llewellyn.com, select your books, and order them on our secure server.

Order by Phone:
- Call toll-free within the U.S. at 1-877-NEW-WRLD (1-877-639-9753). Call toll-free within Canada at 1-866-NEW-WRLD (1-866-639-9753)
- We accept VISA, MasterCard, and American Express

Order by Mail:
Send the full price of your order (MN residents add 7% sales tax) in U.S. funds, plus postage & handling to:

Llewellyn Worldwide
2143 Wooddale Drive, Dept. 1-56718-119-8
Woodbury, MN 55125-2989, U.S.A.

Postage & Handling:

Standard (U.S., Mexico, & Canada). If your order is:
$49.99 and under, add $3.00
$50.00 and over, FREE STANDARD SHIPPING

AK, HI, PR: $15.00 for one book plus $1.00 for each additional book.

International Orders (airmail only):
$16.00 for one book plus $3.00 for each additional book

Orders are processed within 2 business days. Please allow for normal shipping time.
Postage and handling rates subject to change.

The Beginner's Guide to the Recently Deceased

A Comprehensive Travel Guide to the Only Inevitable Destination

DAVID STAUME

Who isn't curious to know what life is like after we die? In this humorous yet thought-provoking glimpse into other realms, David Staume asks you to open your mind and leave your body behind as he takes you on a tour of the "other side."

Find out everything you need to know about the astral realm: how to get around, what's going on, and who and what you might bump into on your travels. Explore the big questions regarding the whys and wherefores of existence: Is there a hell? What about reincarnation? Who am I? Who is God?

0-7387-0426-1
192 pp., 5³⁄₁₆ x 8 $10.95

Write Your Own Magic
The Hidden Power in Your Words

RICHARD WEBSTER

Write your innermost dreams and watch them come true!

This book will show you how to use the incredible power of words to create the life that you have always dreamed about. We all have desires, hopes and wishes. Sadly, many people think theirs are unrealistic or unattainable. *Write Your Own Magic* shows you how to harness these thoughts by putting them to paper.

Once a dream is captured in writing it becomes a goal, and your subconscious mind will find ways to make it happen. From getting a date for Saturday night to discovering your purpose in life, you can achieve your goals, both small and large. You will also learn how to speed up the entire process by making a ceremony out of telling the universe what it is you want. With the simple instructions in this book, you can send your energies out into the world and magnetize all that is happiness, success, and fulfillment to you.

- Send your energies out into the universe with rituals, ceremonies, and spells
- Magnetize yourself so that your desires are attracted to you, while the things you do not want are repelled
- Create suitable spells for different purposes
- Produce quick money, attract a lover, harness the powers of protection, win that job promotion
- Learn the ancient and powerful art of paper-burning, used in the Far East for thousands of years

0-7387-0001-0
5 3/16 x 8, 312 pp. $9.95

To order, call 1-877-NEW WRLD

Prices subject to change without notice

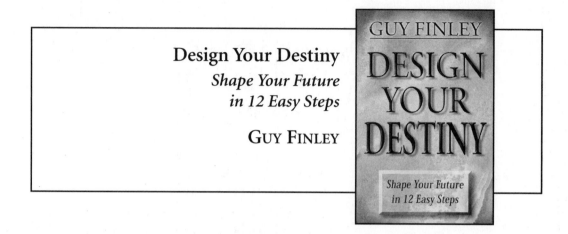

Design Your Destiny
*Shape Your Future
in 12 Easy Steps*

GUY FINLEY

These 12 powerful inner life exercises will help you master the strong and subtle forces that actually determine your life choices and your destiny. You'll discover why so many of your daily choices up to now have been made by default, and how embracing the truth about yourself will banish your self-defeating behaviors forever. Guy Finley reveals and removes many would-be roadblocks to your inner transformation, telling you how to dismiss fear, cancel self-wrecking resentment, quit secret self-sabotage and blaming others for the way you feel.

After reading *Design Your Destiny,* you'll understand why you are perfectly equal to every task you set for yourself, and that you truly can change your life for the better!

1-56718-282-8
216 pp., 5³⁄₁₆ x 8 $9.95

To order, call 1-877-NEW WRLD
Prices subject to change without notice